T0065725

Y2K BUG

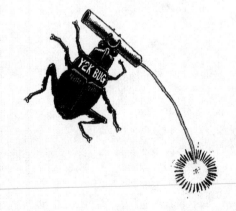

2000
REASONS TO HATE THE
MILLENNIUM

A 21st-Century Survival Guide

Edited by Josh Freed and Terry Mosher

A Fireside Book
Published by Simon & Schuster

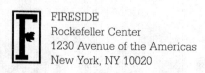

FIRESIDE
Rockefeller Center
1230 Avenue of the Americas
New York, NY 10020

First Fireside Edition 1999
Originally published in Canada by Doubleday Canada Limited

FIRESIDE and colophon are registered trademarks
of Simon & Schuster Inc.

Additional editing by Mike Boone, Jon Kalina, and André Picard
Editorial Coordinator: Janet Torge
Designer: Mary Hughson

Manufactured in the United States of America

1   3   5   7   9   10   8   6   4   2

Library of Congress Cataloging-in-Publication Data is available.
ISBN 0-684-86779-6

There are 1046 book titles that include the word Milleni^Num. 140 of them spell Millenn[∧]ium incorrectly.

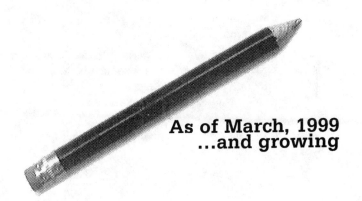

**As of March, 1999
...and growing**

ACKNOWLEDGEMENTS

There weren't quite 2000 people involved in this project but it sometimes felt like it in the whirl of ideas flying over my e-mail during a five-month period. This book is a collaboration of many people, who offered everything from a chapter to a line.

We couldn't have done it without several people who shared the creative workload with Terry and me: editors Mike Boone, Jon Kalina, André Picard and co-ordinator Janet Torge.

They made the book better and they made it fun.

Thanks to all the writers for their contributions, as well as their good humor in adapting to our inexorable demand for more humor. They are: Allen Abel, Byron Ayanoglu, Rick Blue, Mike Boone, George Bowser, Marsha Boulton, Victor Dabby, Scott Feschuk, Charles Gordon, Jon Kalina, Suanne Kelman, Richard King, Mark Lepage, Dave Macdonald, Willa Marcus, Richard Martineau, Alan Mendelsohn, Albert Nerenberg, Cleo Paskal, André Picard, Erika Ritter, Rick Salutin, David Sherman, Jay Stone, Jack Todd, Janet Torge, Josey Vogels and Joel Yanofsky.

More thanks to others who helped out, chief among them McGill University historian, Faith Wallis, who helped me understand when the next Millennium *doesn't* start. Also, Dr. Donna Cherniak for "first child birth of the Millennium" fact-checking. Any errors and exaggeration in either piece are mine alone.

Thanks to volunteer readers Willa Marcus, Victor Dabby and, as always, my wife and colleague, Ingrid Peritz. Thanks to others who offered ideas or help, including Irwin Block, Leslie Orr, Tom Puchniak, Stephen Phizicky and the insta-fact checkers at Torge Ahead.

Finally, much appreciation to editors John Pearce, Christine Innes and the others at Doubleday who shared their time and ideas.

2000 thanks.

Josh Freed

Montreal, March 1, 1999

Josh Freed and I both have day jobs. Therefore, given the five-month window that we had imposed on ourselves to put this book together, it became immediately apparent that we wouldn't be able to deliver the goods without help from many mutually respected colleagues throughout Canada. I'm delighted to say that all of the cartoonists I contacted came through royally.

Starting from the west coast and working east, I would like to thank them all:

> Dan Murphy, *The Vancouver Province*
>
> Graham Harrop, *The Vancouver Sun*
>
> Malcolm Mayes, *The Edmonton Journal*
>
> Dale Cummings, *The Winnipeg Free Press*
>
> Brian Gable, *The Globe and Mail*
>
> Charles Jaffé, *Frank* magazine
>
> Guy Badeaux (a.k.a. Bado), *Le Droit*
>
> Susan Dewar, *The Ottawa Sun*
>
> Serge Chapleau, *La Presse*
>
> Bruce MacKinnon, *The Halifax Herald*

I would also like to thank several illustrators from elsewhere who lent a hand. We managed to chase down Jo Nesbitt, a New York cartoonist, whom we discovered is now living in Amsterdam. Also, during a visit to Montreal from Washington on the last weekend before this book's deadline, Pat Oliphant sat down at our dining room table and drew several wonderful cartoons, thereby filling the final holes in the book.

From Ireland, we received a Millennial limerick (page 153) from author Gordon Snell, along with all best wishes for this project.

Josh and I would also like to express our appreciation to Linda McKnight in Toronto, for giving us counsel on publishing matters.

Most of all, I thank the book's designer – and my partner – Mary Hughson, for constantly keeping things on track.

Terry Mosher (Aislin)

Montreal, March 1, 1998

Table of Contents Countdown...

Forgive them Father, for they will

MILK

the Millennium

Gable

WHY 2K?

10

An Introduction

The Year 2000 will be the biggest birthday bash in human history, but no one knows exactly when, where or what we're celebrating.

Like a car's speedometer hitting 100,000, it's a momentous milestone without meaning.
And everyone seems to be cheering, except you.

WHY 2K ?

Are you suffering from PMSS: Pre-Millennial-Stress Syndrome? Do you cringe when you hear the words, "Millennium Bug?" Do you gag when *Playboy* launches its global search for the Playmate of the Millennium? Do your eyes glaze over when you hear about the newest pre-Millennium trend (kids named Millie), the latest product (New Millennium Toothbrush), or that same question you'll be hearing over and over again:

"So what are YOU doing for the Millennium?"

Are there days when you wish you lived in another era, some time quieter, less disturbing and less, well, Millennial? For instance: Paris during The Terror, or Rome while it was being sacked, or even some inoffensive date in the future like 2079 – long after the Millennium hype is over and a comfortable 921 years before it starts again?

Well, you're not alone. Billions of others are suffering from PMSS too, and for good reason. With less than a year to go before The Moment arrives, the word "Millennial" is already the most over-used adjective of the last 2000 years. And planning for an ordinary New Year's Eve is bad enough – soon you'll be expected to know where you're spending your

Millennium party, who's getting your first Millennial kiss, what your Millennium outfit will be and what Millennium Eve resolutions you'll make.

Suggestion:
"This is definitely my LAST Millennium Eve party."

Then there's the orgy of media-hype you can expect in the final months and days of the countdown. There will be *Time*'s (Hu)man of the Millennium, *Sports Illustrated*'s Athlete of the Millennium, not to mention the Philosopher, the Writer, the Artist, the Butcher, the Baker and the Candlestick-Maker of the Millennium.

There will be TV specials documenting every second of the unfolding celebrations from Aalsmeer, Netherlands to Zywiec, Poland. There will be thousands of Millennium products for sale and billions in government money wasted on the event. There will be no end of talk about the Millennium bug and other Doomsday pests, not to mention the tabloid TV shows before and afterwards:

Jerry Springer:
"RECOVERING MILLENNIUM ADDICTS MEET FIRST-TIME MILLENNIAL MOMS."

By the time it arrives, the Millennium will be the most over-publicized, over-hyped and utterly predictable event of all time; the ultimate opportunity for scamsters, pollsters, psychics, academics, journalists and authors – like us.

So watch out – the Millennium snowball is growing and if you don't do something, it will roll right over you. But what *can* you do?

This book is the answer, your guide to surviving Y2K – the Year 2000 – before it swallows you. It tells you where not to go, how not to dress, even what not to drink on Millennium Eve if you want to miss the Hangover of the Millennium. (Hint: anything with "two thousand flavors" can't be good for you.)

It explains how you can fight back against the Millennium, or ignore it, or postpone it. It even tells you how to miss the Millennium entirely.

In short, this book is a way of getting through the Millennium without dying of boredom first. It will take the stress out of your PMSS.

In addition, and at no extra charge, it gives you at least 2000 reasons to hate the Millennium, though we're sure you can think of lots more. So don't wait another millisecond, start taking control of *your* Millennium right now.

If you like, you can make your first anti-Millennium statement by burning this book.

After you've paid for it, of course.

Josh Freed

THINGS WE THOUGHT WOULD LAST 2000 YEARS THAT DIDN'T

by Marsha Boulton

- Water-walking
- Frankincense and myrrh
- Fish on Fridays

Murphy

- Lighthouse keepers
- Latin teachers
- Mail delivery
- Needing sex for conception
- Eating beef
- Eating
- Smoking
- DDT
- The U.S.S.R.
- The Royal Family
- The family
- Babe Ruth's record
- Booze
- Letter writing
- Reading
- Bank tellers
- Compassion
- Tanning
- Ozone

THINGS WE DIDN'T THINK WOULD LAST UNTIL 2000 THAT MADE A COMEBACK

- Condoms
- Tuberculosis
- Bearded messiahs
- Sandals
- Cigars
- Polyester
- Bellbottoms
- Spike heels and platform shoes

Harrop

- The Volkswagen Beetle
- Tattoos
- Boxer shorts
- Underwire bras
- Joe Clark
- John Glenn
- Bleached hair and dark roots
- Celibacy

IMMORTAL LINES OF THE LAST 2000 YEARS THAT, IN RETROSPECT, WEREN'T

"No sane man will dance."
Cicero

"Rome will never fall."
Anonymous

"The sun never sets
on the British Empire..."
John Wilson, 1829

"This was the war to end all wars."
Woodrow Wilson, after WWI

"Peace in our time."
Neville Chamberlain, before WW II

"Who the hell wants to hear actors talk?"
H. M. Warner, founder of Warner Brothers, 1927

"Computers may weigh no more
than 1.5 tons."
Popular Mechanics, 1949

"We don't like their sound. Guitar groups
are on the way out."
*Decca record executive, 1962, as he refused to sign
The Beatles*

"We will bury you!"
Nikita Kruschev (1894-1971) on capitalism

"Everything that can be invented
has been invented."
*Charles H. Duell,
Commissioner, US Office of Patents, 1899*

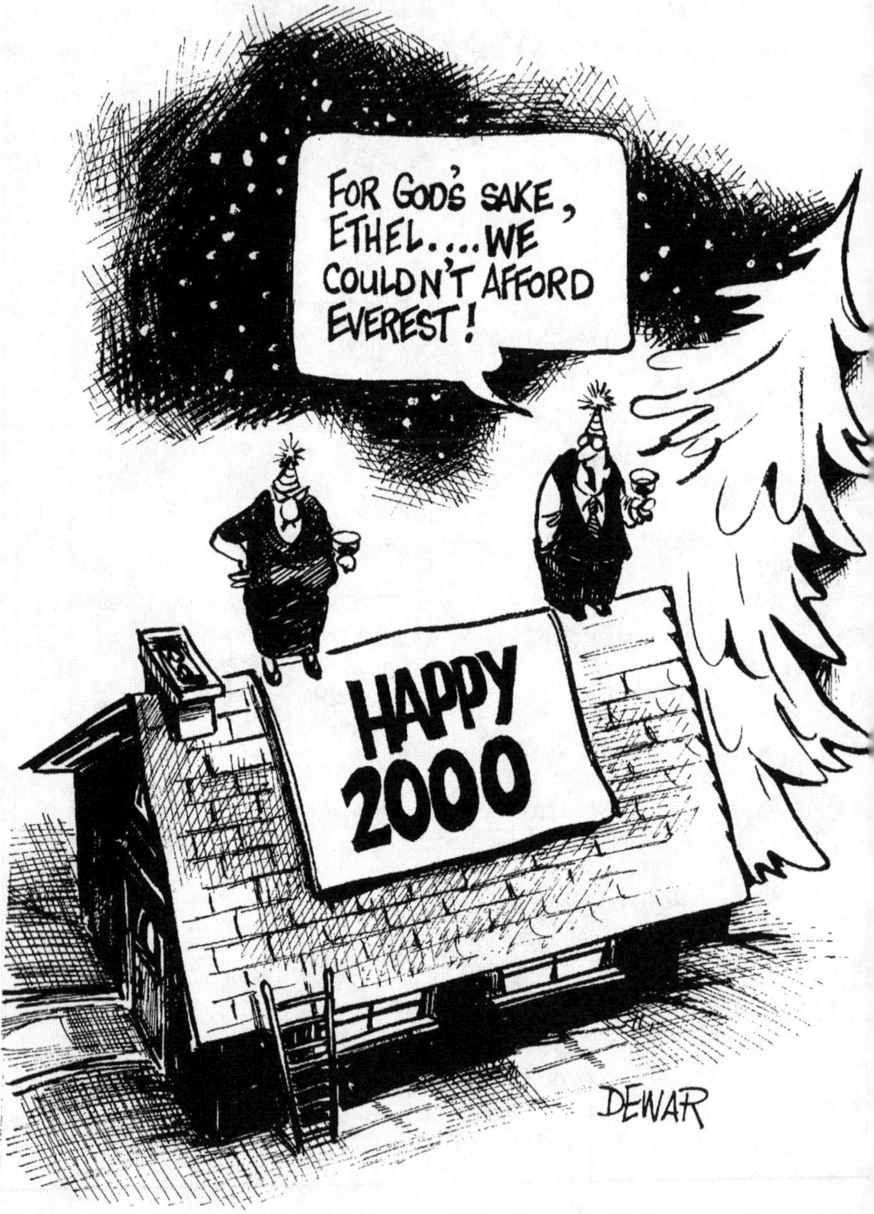
FOR GOD'S SAKE, ETHEL....WE COULDN'T AFFORD EVEREST!
HAPPY 2000
DEWAR

Gable

2K OR NOT 2K?

CHAPTER

9

Where not to celebrate the Millennium

Looking for someplace quiet to escape all the hoopla on Dec. 31, 1999: a remote spot away from the crowds and the madness?

Sorry, the planet is fully booked. Every island, atoll and mountain-top is competing to become the spot to celebrate "the moment." Even if you find a deserted beach on a secluded island in the Pacific, you'll probably be interrupted at 11 p.m., Dec. 31, when a Concorde jet disgorges hordes of Club Med tourists wearing "Hands Up for the Millennium" T-shirts.

19

Here is a guide to the most hyped parties in the world, all competing to be the official Millennium Bash. It will help you figure out where NOT to be on Dec. 31, 1999.

THE CROWDED PLANET GUIDE TO:

where NOT to go this Millennium

by Josh Freed (with Janet Torge and Cleo Paskal)

Jaffé

THE SOUTH PACIFIC

This is Ground Zero – home of the international dateline, where Jan. 1, 2000 strikes first. Several nations are competing for "first-sunrise-of-the-Millennium." The chief contenders are:

THE KINGDOM OF TONGA

Only 100 miles from the dateline, this tiny state staked first claim to be the first-country-to-enter-the-Millennium. Tongans were so confident they built an International Dateline Hotel to accommodate all the tourists...

But then...

THE REPUBLIC OF KIRIBATI...

pulled a fast one. While farther from the dateline than Tonga, these islands straddle two time zones. At least they did until 1995, when the Kiribati government declared the whole country had only one time zone – the earlier one.

This allowed its western islands to celebrate the Millennium an hour before Tonga – and an hour before it actually arrives – at 11 p.m. Dec. 31, 1999.

They also re-named one of their islands Millennium Island – and declared Kiribati would be the first country to see "the dawn of the Millennium."

An angry Tonga complained to the U.N., which could not reverse Kiribati's decision. So the tenacious Tongans have come up with a PR campaign of their own. Tonga has proclaimed it will be "the first kingdom to enter the Millennium."

So there.

Other near-the-dateline nations have also come up with strategies to merchandise their Millennial moment.

GISBORNE, NEW ZEALAND...

claims it will be the "first city to see the sun rise on the Millennium."

WELLINGTON, NEW ZEALAND...

says it will be the "first *major* city to enter the Millennium."

THE CHATHAM ISLANDS...

off New Zealand, will be "the first inhabited land mass" to greet the Millennium dawn.

THE BALLENY ISLANDS...

in Antarctica have been blessed as the site of the "official dawn of the Millennium" by the Royal Greenwich Observatory. They are desolate and uninhabited, so the first being to see the sun rise on the year 2000 will probably be a penguin.

SAMOA...

missed out on the "first dawn" market, because it is a few miles on the wrong side of the dateline. They've made the best of a bad hand by declaring themselves to be the "last place to see the sun set on the old Millennium."

TONGA FIGHTS BACK...

Meanwhile, Tonga is considering going to Daylight Saving Time to catch back up to Kiribati. They've launched a new PR campaign: "The Millennium starts with us."

**If you must go somewhere,
why not get off the beaten track
and come to**

THE NORTH POLE

**This is where all 24 time zones
converge and it's every hour of the day
at the same time.**

You can't miss being the first to greet the year 2000.

If you can make it here, you're guaranteed
to avoid the crowd and have an absolutely unique
Millennium experience. But don't expect to see the
"first light of the Millennium."
Or any light at all – at least until March.

On Dec. 31, it will be pitch dark on the polar ice,
with the Millennium Moment midnight
temperature plunging to
- 80 degrees.

Bring candles.
Watch out for polar bears.

NEWS ITEM: THE CRAFTY ISLANDERS OF PUGA-WUGA WILL BE TOWED 896 MILES EASTWARD IN THE PACIFIC, TO GUARANTEE THEY ARE FIRST TO GREET Y2K...

MORE PLACES NOT TO GO

THE GREAT PYRAMID:

It's booked solid for camel ride tour packages that include Millennium Eve in a tent and a free palm reading ($3035 pp). No alcohol, but perhaps some local extremists will join revelers to celebrate the Millennium in a last burst of glory.

MOROCCO:

Dining à la Sahara, only $6550, entertained by Berber dancers making 50 cents an hour.

FIJI:

It's building a "Millennium Wall" along the dateline, which should make things as peaceful as living next to the Great Wall of China when it was under construction in the 12th century. It will be lit up to be seen from outer space.

NORWAY:

Four artists will be painting the entire town of Sortland blue – as though anyone will know the difference under all the snow.

SOUTH AFRICA:

A 24-hour psychedelic-trance concert in Capetown. On the plus side, they won't hear the countdown.

ENGLAND:

They've gone Millennium-mad. In Greenwich, they will unveil a billion-dollar Millennium Dome at the stroke of midnight. In London, they're building the world's highest Ferris wheel and hiring 10,000 bell ringers to ring the city's 1,200 unused church bells. Trafalgar Square will host a giant gathering of nudists on Millennium Eve – a kind of Full Millennium Monty. It will be preceded by a "full un-dress rehearsal" in June 1999.

THE REST OF EUROPE:

Balloons will be distributed all over the continent in the last months of 1999, for $5 a pop. Hundreds of millions of people will put a message in them, fill them up with helium and let them go at the big moment. It's one more reason not to fly on Dec. 31, 1999.

ANYWHERE IN CALIFORNIA:

A million people will gather in the desert to chant at the stroke of midnight in a Pagan Festival. Levitation is optional.

YES, IT'S FINALLY SAFE TO GO TO IRELAND

The big moment was to be announced by a huge sunken clock counting down the moments at the bottom of the Liffey River. At midnight, it would erupt in fireworks and rise from the deep to signal the new age.

However, it will have to wait for 3000. Soon after the clock was installed, algae were attracted by its light, turning the display into a fuzzy, yellow haze. Eventually Dublin scrapped the $500,000 contraption, though locals still recall it fondly as the "chime in the slime."

Chapleau

IF YOU PREFER SOMETHING MORE SPIRITUAL, THE PLACE TO AVOID IS THE VATICAN:

Some 4 million people are expected for the Grand Jubilee during the Year 2000. As very long lineups are anticipated, the Holy Father will be working overtime to hear End-of-Millennium Confession. To expedite matters, the Vatican will also be receiving confessions by e-mail.

Send all sins to holyfather@vatican.god

Or telephone: 1-800-DIAL-A-SIN.

- Press 1 for MORTAL
- Press 2 For VENIAL

If you do not know the status of your sin, Press O and consult our Directory of Sins.

MILLENNIUMBEGONE

**Tired of hearing about Millennium bugs and other pests?
Wish you could just forget the whole thing?**

Then come to the **MILLENNIUM-FREE FARM!**

*From the moment
you arrive, you'll forget the you-know-what
because you-won't-know-when it is.*

- We'll confiscate your watch, calendar and agenda
- We'll remove all Millennium news from your papers
- We'll bleep out any mention of it on TV, with our patented M-chip
- Even your checks will be undated (except the one you give us)

We'll make sure you have an M-proof holiday.

After the big moment has come and gone,
you'll be rested and ready to face the next 1000 years.

You'll never know what you missed.

Millennium-Free Farm — It s About Time.

**CAMP MILLENNIUMBEGONE, 1000 Islands, Ontario, Y2K NOT
Call toll free: 1-800-TIME-OUT**

**Ask about our Millennium-recovery programs
and Millennium-detox camps for your family and friends**

WHO'S NOT CELEBRATING?

We constantly hear about the people who are celebrating the Millennium – but what about those who aren't? Is there any way to join them? Yes! To forget the Millennium completely, all you have to do is convert to a religion that's NOT celebrating the Year 2000. For instance, you could become...

A HASSIDIC JEW

The Good News: On Jan. 1, 2000, you'll be living in the year 5760, so you won't have to worry about the next Millennium for another 240 years – in Y6K.

The Bad News: You have to wear black, and you will be very bad at parking.

AN AYMARA INDIAN IN BOLIVIA

Good News: You celebrate New Year's on winter solstice, in mid-December, when no one is partying apart from the odd Druid. Plus you're living in the year 5508.

Bad News: Everyone has to wear one of those funny Bolivian hats and travel around the world playing flute music in subway stations.

A MUSLIM

Good News: On Jan. 1, 2000, it will be 1420, so you don't have to worry about celebrating the Millennium for nearly 600 years. In some places, like Afghanistan, try celebrating before that and they'll put you in jail for heresy.

Bad News: The year 1500 is coming up in just under a century.

Aislin

A CITIZEN OF INDIA

Good News: You have a range of religions and years to choose from. For example, it will be Buddha Year 2542, Kali Year 5102, Vikrama Year 2055 and Shaka Year 1921. In fact, only about 2.5% of India's population are Christians who officially celebrate the Millennium.

Bad News: That's still a *LOT* of people.

A CITIZEN OF CHINA

Good News: More than a billion people aren't celebrating the Millennium, which makes it easy to ignore.

Bad News: Half of them are working in factories making Millennium trinkets to sell to the rest of us.

A CITIZEN OF SAN MARINO

Good News: This tiny microstate, near Italy's Adriatic coast, has its own calendar system that started when the country was founded Sept. 3, 301 A.D. That means it will only be 1698, so you have another two years to go before San Marino throws its next centennial bash.

Bad News: They celebrate it with their annual New Year's Eve tradition – a nation-wide bingo game.

WHOSE HOLIDAY IS IT?

If you think about it, most of the world will not celebrate the coming Millennium. Only 33% of the planet's population will – Judaeo-Christian countries that use the Christian calendar.

IN SHORT, THE MILLENNIUM IS
AN ETHNIC HOLIDAY.

So if you don't want to convert, try this special Millennium conversation stopper! The next time someone asks you the Dreaded Question:

"So what are YOU doing on the Millennium?"

Just say: "Nothing. Don't you know that celebrating the Millennium is culturally insensitive and Eurocentric? The whole thing is just a marketing conspiracy by the western world to impose its calendar system on everyone else."

"I'm boycotting it."

MISSING THE MOMENT

(When not to celebrate)

by Josh Freed

You may *think* the official Millennium Moment is the instant that midnight, Dec. 31, 1999, turns to Jan. 1, 2000 – and billions of people all over the world turn to give their partner "a kiss across two Millennia."

But don't believe everything you hear. Despite the mass marketing of the Moment, no one actually knows when the next Millennium starts. And Jan. 1, 2000 is one of the least plausible dates.

Let's look at a few alternatives, so you can choose the Millennial moment you want. After all, how can you avoid celebrating it, if you don't know when it happens?

THEORY 1: IT'S JAN. 1, 2001

This is the most popular candidate for when the next millennium really starts. It's even been adopted by Australians, who plan to celebrate a year later.

Their thinking is that since there was no Year Zero, we started our calendar system in January of the Year 1 and lost a whole year. That means Jan. 1, 2000 is actually Jan. 1, 1999, and we don't hit the Millennium until Jan. 1, 2001.

This theory makes some sense mathematically, but we don't recommend it. Otherwise, like Australians, you'll have to put up with a whole extra year of pre-Millennium hype.

THEORY 2: IT'S DEC. 25, 1999

That's Jesus' birthday, and isn't that what we're celebrating – 2000 years since the birth of Christ?

The fact is Jan. 1 is just a leftover holiday from pre-Christ days – when it was ancient Rome's annual New Year's Eve bash. The Romans called it "the Holiday Of Fools," and got roaring drunk, dressed up in silly clothing and presumably counted down "X...IX...VIII...VII...VI..."

The Roman Catholic church spent centuries arguing (unsuccessfully) that New Year's Day be moved to Dec. 25 – the "real" start of Christian time.

If you buy this theory, then you should celebrate the Millennium on Christmas Day, with a kiss under the mistletoe.

But there's a flaw in this thinking too, because there's no evidence that Christ was born Dec. 25. So, when was He born?

THEORY 3: LATER THAN THAT

Face it – there were no birth certificates or driver's licenses in Christ's time. Church officials eventually chose Dec. 25th to celebrate his birthday, because it coincided with other holidays around the winter equinox.

But the date is thought to be way off.

According to the Bible, Jesus was born "while shepherds tended their flocks by night." They couldn't have done this in December, in Judea, or there'd have been a lot of shivering sheep and frost-bitten shepherds.

More likely it was during "lambing season" which took place in early March. This would mean the next Millennium actually starts about Mar. 1, 2000.

Or…

THEORY 4: EARLIER THAN THAT

According to the Bible, the three wise men who visited baby Jesus were sent by King Herod. But Herod died in 4 B.C. – or four years *Before Christ.*

How could Jesus have been born Before Christ?

More likely, the calendar is off by four years. That would mean the Year 0 happened at least four years earlier, and the Year 2000 happened in 1996.

Does this mean you should cancel your Dec. 31 party plans?

Not until you hear some more possible dates for the start of the Millennium.

THEORY 5: IT WAS EVEN EARLIER THAN THAT

The best historic clue to Christ's birthday is that bright "little star of Bethlehem" the three wise men supposedly followed. Many scholars think the "star" was probably an astronomical phenomenon that took place around the time Christ was born.

Scientists say that a major celestial event took place in that era: a brilliant supernova caused by an exploding star – in 6 or 7 B.C. Many believe this is the best bet for the real year of Jesus' birth, and the real Year 0 in our calendar.

Which means the new Millennium could have begun 7 years ago, in 1993.

There's a small problem with this theory too: it makes Jesus at least 39 when he died, not 33, as Luke claims in the Bible. Is it possible Jesus was a very young-looking 40, or did he just lie about his age?

THEORY 6: IT WAS BOTH EARLIER AND LATER

Our calendar system was updated in 1582. Until then, it didn't have leap years built in, so spring equinox had gradually fallen more than a week behind the Mar. 21 date on the calendar.

And lambing season was probably colliding with spring cleaning.

To get the calendar back on schedule, Pope Gregory XIII announced "The Great Correction." People went to sleep on Oct. 4, 1582 and woke up 11 days later on Oct. 15.

This corrected the calendar, but also meant we lost 10 days. Which means the Millennium happens 10 days later.

So, you can choose any theory you want and celebrate or ignore the Millennium accordingly. Or you can add all the theories up to get the best estimate of the Right Date.

Y2K = 7 years earlier than we thought, because that's when Jesus was really born, plus a year later for the year we lost skipping Year Zero, minus 9 months because He wasn't born in December, but in March, when shepherds tended their flocks by night, plus 10 days for the Great Correction when we all lost over a week's sleep we could still use today.

Therefore, the new Millennium actually started on Mar. 11, 1994.

Congratulations! You can sleep right through Dec. 31, 1999 without worrying about missing The Millennium – because you've already missed it.

The Bible tells us so.

Then again, the whole calendar system is such a shaky mess, no one knows for sure. In truth, you can declare the Millennium to be almost any day you want – and you'll have as good a chance of being right as anyone else.

And a better chance than all the people pushing Jan. 1, 2000 countdown watches.

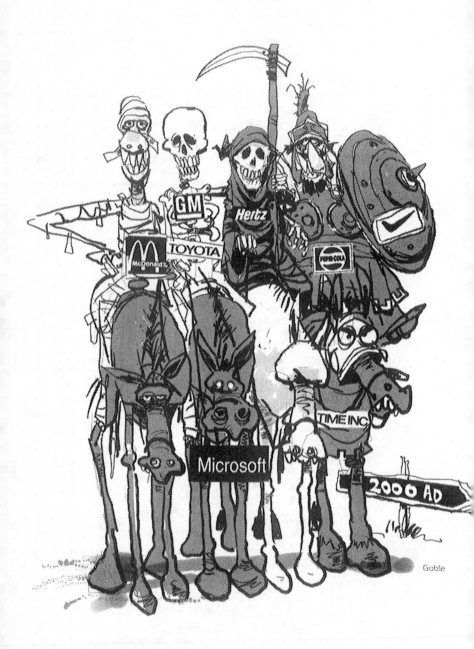

THE FOUR HORSEMEN OF THE MILLENNIUM

Gable

THE Y2 K–MART

Merchandising The Millennium

Luxury hotels have been taking reservations for Dec. 31, 1999 for almost two decades. So have many swanky restaurants.

Almost half a billion bottles of champagne have been ordered for Millennium Eve celebrations and just as many bottles of Tylenol for the next morning.

Never mind fun. The Year 2000 means a once-in-a-thousand-year opportunity for profit...

MERCHANDISING THE MILLENNIUM

by André Picard

As predictable as the tick-tick-tick of the Millennium clock counting down is the drip-drip-drip of entrepreneurs salivating at the money to be made from Millennium shlock.

Thousands of Year 2000 products are flooding the market from countdown watches to Millennium cars, snowblowers, toothbrushes and leg waxes. For $2,000 you can even buy yourself a stainless steel Millennium funeral casket.

Companies have laid claim to being the official car, official hamburger, official light bulb, official binoculars, official ballast, official vending machine and "Official intellectual property law firm" of the Millennium.

Korbel Champagne Co. is spending a whopping $25-million to promote its "Official Champagne of the Millennium." At the other end of the gourmet spectrum, Snickers has applied to be the "Official Candy of the New Millennium." Not to be outdone, M & M took out the copyright on MM – the Roman numerals for 2000.

Nothing is too inconsequential to be Millennial. The makers of Millennium 2000 Pesticide hope their new company name will create some buzz. Says their president: "I think people want to participate in the next Millennium and we're trying to help them do it."

By killing 2000 cockroaches?

Are we consumers as dumb as these guys think? Will we all be stockpiling kitchen scraps for our newly-purchased Compost 2000? Plowing our way

through winter with the Snowblaster 2000? Reeling in the big ones with the Fishing Tackle of the New Millennium?

Bloomingdale's has opened a whole Millennium department for customers eager to drop 2000 bucks in a millisecond. It features must-have products like Millennium Night renewal cream, which you'll want to keep tucked away in your Chanel 2005 handbag, a "body-friendly" purse that costs a wallet-unfriend-ly $2,000.

Can the Mc2000 burger be far away?

Thousands of Products Have Millennium Trade Marks. They Include...

- Mazda Millenial car (their spelling)
- La-Z-Boy Millennia office chairs
- 3rd Millennium Rope
- Jubilee – The Coffee for the Millennium
- Millie: The genuine Millennium Bug
- Milly The Millennium Bear
- Molly: The third Millennium doll
- Millennium Schmillennium
- The Millennium Flower
- New Millennium Steaks
- New Millennium Bible
- Fishing Tackle of the New Millennium
- The Watchdog for the Millennium
- Microwave Popcorn for the New Millennium
- Air Freshener for the New Millennium
- Pet Food of the Millennium
- Toothbrush for the New Millennium
- Uncle Ben's, The Food of the Millennium
- Beefeater Live A Little, The Official Martini of the Millenium (yes, they spelled it wrong)
- Millenium Ale (ditto)
- Magic Millenium Moment (oops again)
- Magic Millennium Moment
  (guess somebody finally got spell-check)

"2000" PRODUCTS
TO EXPECT

- Christmas lights sold in strands of 2000
- Lipo-suction Barbie
- Alzheimer Ken
- A line of children's Millennium swaddling clothes with the logo "J.C."
- Vanity plates ending Y2K
- Sunblock 2000

MOVIE SEQUELS

- *Rocky 2000*
- *How to Marry a Millenniumaire*
- *Dial M for Millennium*
- *H$_2$000*
- *3001: A Space Oddity*

BOOKS

- *Millennium for Dummies*
- *The Man who Mistook his Wife for the Millennium*
- *A Tale of Two Millennia*
- *The Millennia on the Floss*

SONGS

- "I'm Dreaming of a Y2K Christmas"
- "You're 2016, You're Beautiful and You're Mine"
- "Will You Still Love Me When I'm 64K?"
- "2000 Ways to Leave Your Lover"
- "It's Been a Hard Day's Millennium Night"

MILLENNIUM TRAVEL FOR THE VERY RICH

Save a fortune. Take our advice and avoid the following junkets, being offered to the super-rich:

SUCKER JUNKET #1

For $100,000 per couple, you can get a suite at any Ritz hotel along with "two matching 18-carat gold watches, a Jaguar for the weekend, 24-hour butler service, a magnum of Tattinger's, daily massages, engraved stationery," upscale toiletries and, we hope, a big sign to wear around your neck saying: "1st sucker of the new Millennium."

SUCKER JUNKET #2

For $70,000 per person, you can take an around-the-world flight on a Concorde jet racing the sun. The sponsors promise that you'll get to celebrate Millennium Eve at Heathrow airport, then again as you fly over the Atlantic, and finally when you land in New York, just in time to mark the big moment again – at JFK airport.

INSTEAD, IF YOU'RE THAT RICH, WHY NOT USE THE MONEY TO AVOID THE MILLENNIUM? HERE'S IDEA #3

Fly a Concorde the other direction, delaying the Millennium's arrival as long as possible. If timed right, you'll miss the Millennium moment in every time zone, stay in 1999 until the last possible instant, then cross the dateline in time to miss the day entirely!

You'll go directly from Dec. 31, 1999 to Jan. 2, 2000.
Congratulations – you've missed the Millennium!

Cummings

A VIRGIN POLICY

According to London's *Evening Standard*, an insurance company in England, GRIP, has sold over 1000 policies to women who want protection against a virgin birth during the Millennium. The policy costs a 100 pounds a year and pays 1,000,000 pounds. So if you do have the next Messiah, at least you'll be able to afford diapers for the baby and therapy for yourself.

THE STATE'S STAKE
Government Meets The Millennium

BEING Y2K-BUG-COGNIZANT, MR. MALOWSKI IS ASKING THAT, RATHER THAN SENDING HIM HIS MONTHLY GOVERNMENT CHECK, WE GIVE HIM GOLD INSTEAD...

Where business dares to go, government dares to follow – eventually. Some corporations started their Year 2000 plans as early as 1967, but most governments discovered the possibilities only recently.

They're making up for lost time with grandiose projects. The British government's new Millennium Commission has a whopping $3.2 billion budget. The centerpiece of the celebrations is the $1.2 billion-dollar Millennium Dome, billed as the "21st century Stonehenge."

Wales is constructing a futuristic $46 million rugby stadium.

The French government is refurbishing every major building from Paris to Nice, and will build the world's "longest hedge," from Calais to Carcassonne. One agency will release thousands of perfumed multicolored fish into the Seine.

Even the poor Eiffel Tower has a neon sign counting down the days to Jan. 1, 2000, when it will broadcast pictures of a giant electronic egg being hatched.

German funsters will mark the Millennium with a passion play about the life of Christ. Australia, while clinging stubbornly to the idea the 21st century doesn't begin until 2001, will spend $3.4 billion on the 2000 Olympic Sydney Games.

Canada's Millennium Bureau is spending more than $145 million on nation-affirming projects. These include an all-Canadian baseball museum – okay, so it will be small – and a bold plan to build the world's largest dinosaur atop the tourist office in Drumheller, Alberta.

Visitors will be able to climb into the $250,000 beast and stare out its mouth, the view of the Canadian Prairies being far more spectacular from the second floor than the first.

The U.S. was a bit slow off the mark, but has made up for lost time by having vice-president Al Gore utter the word "Millennium" every time he speaks. The government has also created a White House Millennium Council, where America's greatest minds can debate the momentous philosophical issues of the Millennium Eve, such as: "How many red, how many white and how many blue fireworks should we buy?"

The council has also dispersed about $30 million to cultural endeavors like the Millennium Mobile, which is touring the country to film ordinary Americans on the eve of the 21st century, then re-broadcasting it to other ordinary Americans on the vehicle's giant video screen.

America's Unfunniest Homes Videos

The Smithsonian Institution is also working to restore the original Star Spangled Banner, though it admits the Millennium project won't be complete until at least 2001. However, the alterations on Uncle Sam's pants will be ready on Monday.

Meanwhile, the President has announced that the bridge to the next Millennium will be temporarily delayed due to budget cuts.

Governments in all countries will pay for their Millennium projects the same way. Shortly after the dawn of the new age, finance ministers around the world will rise up to say that, due to the economic crisis caused by Y2K, there is little choice but to institute a temporary levy – not a tax! – on the Millennium.

It will last 1000 years.

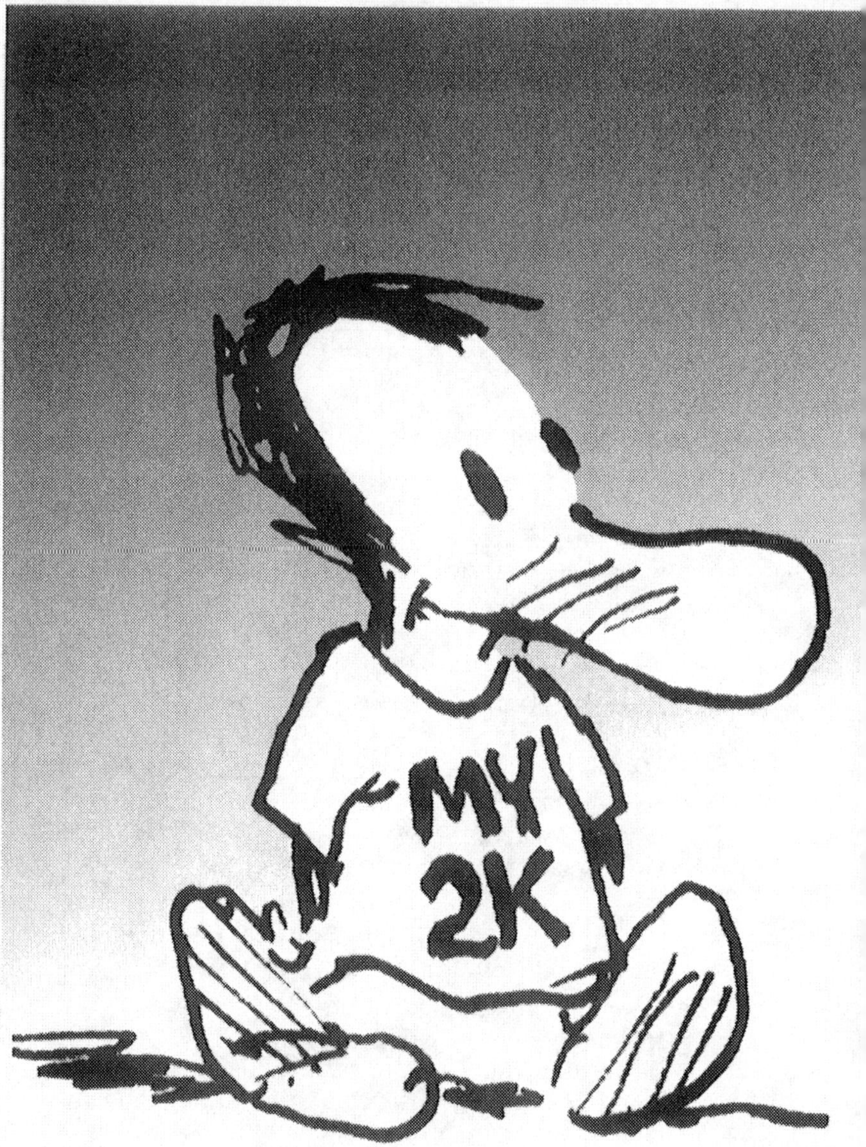
MY
2K
Oliphant

Gable

Y NOT U2?

How to make this your Millennium

2000 years ago it was hard to make your messianic mark on a new Millennium. Even if you did, it was a risky business with little recognition until after death.

But this Millennium there's plenty of opportunity for anyone with a message and a little media savvy. Many people are already staking their claim to the next 1000 years – or at least their fifteen minutes of it.

So get in line, before it's too late.

abraham BEGAT issac;
and issac BEGAT jacob; and
jacob BEGAT judas and his brethren;
and judas BEGAT phares, and zara of thamar;
and phares BEGAT esrom;
and esrom BEGAT aram;
and aram BEGAT aminadab; and
aminadab BEGAT naasson; and
naasson BEGAT salmon;
and salmon BEGAT booz of rachab;
and booz BEGAT obed of ruth;
and obed BEGAT jesse; and
jesse BEGAT david the king; and
david the king BEGAT solomon of her that had been the wife of
urias; and solomon BEGAT roboam; and
roboam BEGAT abia;
and abia BEGAT asa;
asa BEGAT josaphat;
josaphat BEGAT joram;
and joram BEGAT ozias; and
ozias BEGAT joatham; and
joatham BEGAT achaz;
and achaz BEGAT ezekias;
and ezekias BEGAT manasses;
and manasses BEGAT amon; and
amon BEGAT josias;
and josias BEGAT jechonias ... thren, about the time
they were carried away to babylon; and ... e carried away
to babylon jechonias BEGAT salathiel;
and salathiel BEGAT zorobabel;
zorobabel BEGAT abiud; and
abiud BEGAT eliakim;
and eliakim BEGAT azor;
and azor BEGAT sadoc; and
sadoc BEGAT achim;
and achim BEGAT eliud;
and eliud BEGAT eleazar;
eleazar BEGAT matthan;
and matthan BEGAT jacob;
and jacob BEGAT joseph;
and God said, "STOP FUCKING AROUND!"

INNER MESSIAH MILLENNIAL TOURS

by Victor Dabby

Do you ever wake up in the morning, look in the mirror and ask: "Do I have a calling? Is my life meant to be more meaningful?"

"Could I be... the Messiah?"

Welcome to the club.

You've got the Jerusalem Syndrome, the deeply held belief that you're The One. And you're not the Only One. As the Millennium approaches, more and more people are coming out of the closet to announce that they too are "the Son of God." (Or the Daughter of the Divinity.)

It's Millennial messianic mania, an exciting new movement of doomsday devotees and apocalyptic new agers. And don't scoff. Maybe they're onto something.

Maybe the Messiah *is* coming at the stroke of midnight, New Year's Eve, 1999, J.L.T. (Jerusalem Local Time).

In fact, maybe he's already among us.

And maybe, just maybe, you're Him!

Isn't it time you found out with: Messiah Tours – Jerusalem's leading experts at finding the Inner Messiah in you?

"But how can I be the Messiah?" you ask. "I'm only... a carpenter." You could do worse.

Here at Messiah Tours, we have clients from all walks of life: accountants, backpackers, ex-priests and many, many dentists who all think they are Him. And they'll all be gathering in the Holy Land this Millennium Eve to find out if they're right.

Don't miss the messianic boat. This Christmas, come on down to Jerusalem, a town with a proven track record – a town that's been turning out miracles for millennia.

Who can forget Jesus and Joseph, Peter and Paul, David and Solomon? – all satisfied customers of Jerusalem! Remember the "Sermon on the Mount?" Well, that was one of our workshops, and we put the town of Armageddon on the map.

Awesome.

At Messiah Tours, we have room for false messiahs, near messiahs and missing messiahs – not to mention the real McCoy, which could mean you!

We even offer a special pre-Millennium tour:

Try our

SPECIAL MESSIAH PACKAGE

Includes a crown of thorns, an authentic manger and a white donkey with unlimited mileage. We'll also organize the multitudes for you and throw in a staff, Birkenstocks and a free visit from any Three Wise Men of your choice.

Messiah-hood is one percent inspiration and 99 percent perspiration. So let us do the work. If you have back problems, we can have someone else carry your cross.

To help find your Inner Messiah, we offer many courses:

- **Water-Walking in Three Easy Steps (left, right, left).**
- **Our ever-popular EZ Multiplying Loaves and Fishes mix.**
- **Raising the dead at a local cemetery of your choice.**

(Batteries not included)

The athletically-minded can sign up for our Trinity Triathlon: a sprint down the Via Dolorosa, followed by Upper Body Cross-Lifting on Calvary Hill and Speed Nail-hammering. At the end of the day, we cater an excellent Last Supper.

So why settle for a normal life, when you could be immortal? With any luck you'll found a religion and have your picture over a million mantles.

Book now for your stay at the Messianic Mission Motel. All rooms double-occupancy/shared with one or more disciples.

Only $2000
(not including airfare, room or halo).

The official kickoff of the first Millennium,
as every fan of Christianity knows, was the arrival of the
Messiah. What they don't know is that the Savior of Mankind
had company on his fateful journey down the birth canal.
Read about this amazing revelation in...

CHRIST HAD A TWIN SISTER!!!

The Untold Story

by Erika Ritter

Gable

THE MISSING MISSIAH

DON'T SHOOT THE MISSENGER

Contrary to popular belief, Jesus was not an only holy child. He had a twin sister, The Missiah. Or, to be politically correct, the MS. IAH, delivered of the same Virgin Mother that very same night, in the same stable on the outskirts (N.B. "skirts") of Bethlehem.

Even more surprisingly, the Virgin Mary herself may have been part of the conspiracy to keep her Divine Daughter's star from shining as brightly as her Son's.

Evidence suggests that instead of being allowed to learn showy skills such as raising the dead, the Missiah was confined to dull domestic tasks like raising bread. And while her Beatific Bro was going about his Father's business of turning water into wine, his Celestine Sis was busy turning beaten egg whites into Mary's Miraculous Fool-Proof Angel Food Cake.

Chapleau

By the end of Christ's ministry, the rift between the Holy Mother, the Holy Sister and the rest of the Holy Family had widened into a Holy War. This explains the Missiah's absence from the famous portrait of The Last Supper – painted presumably while She was out in the kitchen washing up The Last Dishes to serve The Last Dessert.

After Christ's crucifixion, the Missiah tried to support herself by riding on her brother's robetails. A school for hockey goaltenders ("Jesus Saves, And You Can Too!") failed in less than a season. Also doomed was a pedicure salon the

Missiah set up with Mary Magdalene, who turned off many customers by drying their freshly-anointed feet with her hair.

The Missiah's biggest business fiasco was her ill-advised effort to launch the first talk radio network, specializing in phone-ins with the angry and disgruntled. It was known as The Stations of the Cross.

MILLENNIUM OR MALE-ENNIUM?

For whatever reason it happened, the Missiah's failure led to a largely male cast for the coming 2,000 years. Major male contributions to civilization include: syphilis, the thumbscrew, the Barcalounger, droit-de-seigneur, beer, bear-baiting, tail fins, the 19th hole, high-fives and the dunking stool.

Suppressed in her own time, derided by her twin, ignored by her Father, and sold out by her mother, the Savior's twin sister still managed to exert some much-needed female influence on the course of human history. Even a quick comparison serves to drive this home:

WHERE THE BOYS ARE		WHY HEAVEN THANKS LITTLE GIRLS
L. Ron Hubbard	☞	Mother Hubbard
The Rat Pack	☞	The mudpack
The Stanley Cup	☞	The D Cup
Gone Fishin'	☞	Gone with the Wind
Hostile Take-over	☞	Apple Turnover
Ozone	☞	Erogenous zone
Pound out	☞	Pound cake
Weightlift	☞	Facelift
Pennzoil	☞	Oil of Olay
Newt Gingrich	☞	Fig Newton

TOWARD A HAPPIER HERSTORY

If the third millennium is heralded by the Second Coming, it is clearly the Missiah who will return, NOT her better-known Brother. Women not only come more readily than men, they come more often.

Thus, the next Millennium will logically boast a gentler female emphasis on conception, creativity, cradling and couture, rather than the ominous auguries of Armageddon that have dominated history since the dawn of the Anno Domini era.

Under the influence of the Missiah, we can look forward to buffing our nails, rather than hammering them, and making whoopee not war, so long as a clean-up committee is firmly in place. The Missiah should also inspire a passion for fashion, more millinery than millennary. Hats will be back, while brickbats will become old hat. As for hemlines... well, that's anyone's guess, in any era.

The only sure bet for the Year 2000 is that all bets are off. Once the computer toys-for-boys have crashed, the asteroids have hurtled to Earth, and all that other bang-bang-you're-dead stuff has been purged from the system, it'll be:

So long, Billy the Kid and hello Nicole Kidman.

Hey Missiah – we've missed ya.

54

IT'S YOUR MILLENNIUM, BABY

A Woman's Guide to Having the Millennium's First Child

by Josh Freed

Coach:
Janet Torge

The race is on to have the first baby of the Millennium, the most talked about birth in 2000 years. The first child to show its face Jan. 1, 2000 will have its future assured. There'll be million-dollar endorsement contracts the moment he or she leaves the womb, photos in the *National Enquirer*, appearances on Oprah, book and movie offers, diaper endorsements, a page in the *Guinness Book of World Records* – maybe even a religion to lead.

Savvy couples have timed their child's birth down to the last second. So why be a spectator? All that's needed is the right egg and the right sperm at the right time — and your child could lead us into the next Millennium.

Even if you haven't gotten started, it may not be too late if you follow our advice. The Millennial Child could still be your child as long as you hurry.

1: TRADITIONAL CONCEPTION:

If you like earth tones and cotton clothing this is your option. The traditional way takes an average of 266.56 days — so counting backwards from Dec. 31 on your day-timer, the perfect time to conceive was Friday, April 16, 1999, at 13:44 p.m.

Smart couples booked the day off well in advance. Why rush home at lunch for a quickie, when you're having a child who will be famous for eternity?

Even if you missed the deadline, you're not necessarily out of the race. With modern technology, you never know how early baby may arrive, so put this book down now and go straight to the bedroom. Miracles only happen to those who make them happen.

MEDIA ADVICE: It's no good having the first baby of the Millennium if nobody knows. Other greedy breeders will be putting in false claims, so it's important to get the media on-side from the start.

As we know from Jesus, conception is a big part of any Millennium baby's story. You'll want a record of your progress for future books, films and CD-ROMS about Him\Her. Your team should include a spin doctor who knows how to use the media to advantage. Bring in the cameras after the first ultrasound, as soon as you know your child's sex. Find an appropriate name (Millie or Len) and put out a press release announcing that your child is in contention for a Dec. 31st birth.

Don't forget to send along photos of the ultrasound – so they can see how cute your kid will be. Say things like, "I know the other parents are good people and it's going to be a tough race — but I'm confident we've got the winning zygote."

2: ARTIFICIAL INSEMINATION

If you drive a BMW and your barbecue has electronic igniters, your birth method of choice is artificial insemination. In-vitro fertilization often produces two or more babies, doubling your chances of having one when the clock strikes midnight.

SCHEDULE: 6 hours fertilization

42 hours of embryo transfer

267.5 days of pregnancy

TOTAL: 269.5 days

One big advantage of this method is the wide choice of fathers. While many women are stuck with their partner's genes, in-vitro lets you select any sperm you want.

Every Millennium has an ideal look. Jesus was just right for the year 0, with his brown hair, brown eyes and cute halo – but this Millennium most competitors are thinking multi-cultural and androgynous. A well-balanced bisexual sports hero is the perfect donor. Or just a sensitive astronaut who plays the piano.

3: MIDNIGHT C-SECTION

You're always late for the movies and you never file your tax returns on time — so a last minute C-section is probably right for you. Even if you got started way behind schedule, you can make up valuable weeks, or months of time. It's also the most reliable way to guarantee a Millennium moment birth.

With a deft surgeon, the time of birth can be controlled down to the last second, which may be what this horse...sorry, baby-race comes down to.

The biggest challenge will be finding a good obstetrics ward for your C-section delivery. Most were booked for Dec. 31 years ago, by competitors who really understood planned parenthood, so you may have to book a bed on another continent where the race is less intense.

Remember – many airlines won't let you fly in the final 10 weeks of pregnancy, so be sure to leave by the Oct. 15 deadline. Planes are already booking up, so don't delay, call your travel agent today.

Once you're travelling abroad, you may want to consider going to the forefront of the baby race – the international dateline, in the South Pacific – where the Millennium arrives first. That way, if you just miss having the first child of this Millennium, you are almost guaranteed to have the last child of the 20th century. Not a bad consolation prize.

We recommend a Millennium cruise boat circling the dateline, which provides good opportunities for tabloid coverage, as in: FIRST BIRTH IN BERTH!!! Don't forget to bring along a snappy sign to catch the eye of passing TV crews in helicopters, such as: MILLENNIUM BABY ON BOARD.

If you're having twins, we suggest the northeast tip of Siberia, which overlaps the dateline. That way you can have your first child just before the clock strikes midnight EST, then roll over and have a second child at exactly 00:00:01 EST.

Even if you just miss, you'll earn your baby a place in the record book as a Child of 2 Millennia. And you'll be remembered as The Mother of all MillenniuMums.

Choose a doctor who is flexible. They should be aware that billions of people will eventually watch this history-making event, because you'll be having it videotaped. Encourage your doctor to replace the traditional "greens" with a more festive outfit, bearing the words "Welcome to the New Century" across the chest.

In the past, kidnappers proved they had their hostages by taking a photo of them holding that day's newspaper. In a similar manner, you should place a TV behind the delivery table, with the Times Square countdown plainly in view.

This way your doctor can deliver the child at the stroke of midnight – though it's important not to block the TV with the emerging baby at the crucial final moment. This could be a photo finish – so you don't want your doctor to hog the shot.

TIP: It's never too early to hire an agent.

Even if your child misses out by a half-second, your agent can find backup options. For instance, you could claim your child is the real Millennium baby and the winner is a false messiah. There's lots of mileage to be had from this angle, as many have shown over the last 2000 years.

At worst, your child can always start a cult.

4: VIRGIN BIRTH

It's quicker and easier – but a tough sell. The story is very old and it's been done to death. You're better off going with something more modern.

MIDNIGHT
DEC. 31, 1999

MacKinnon

Gable

Y BUG ME?

CHAPTER

6

An exterminator's guide

*"The sky is falling.
The sky is falling."*

Chicken Little
How My Sky Fell and Other Poultry Tales

Is the Millennium bug bugging you? Do you wish you could just call an exterminator and stamp it out once and for all? This chapter is for you – your guide to eliminating the most annoying pest of the last 1000 years.

EVERYTHING YOU NEVER WANTED TO KNOW ABOUT THE BUG!

by Jon Kalina

"Gosh! It's just amazing what computers can do nowadays!"

WHAT EXACTLY IS A MILLENNIUM BUG AND WHY SHOULD I WORRY ABOUT IT?

According to computer geeks, almost everything that runs on computers will stop working at the stroke of midnight, Dec. 31, 1999. This includes the government computers that issue your driver's license and pension checks, your car's computerized gas tank and steering wheel, your VCR-plus programming and your automatic can-opener.

Many experts think the Millennium bug will lead to a

global crisis, a worldwide depression and even more terrifying, a blank TV screen. Some survivalists believe it will be the End Of The World As We Know It, and they are hiding out in the Arizona desert stockpiling food, guns and Swiss army knife can-openers.

WHY IS THIS HAPPENING TO ME?

Because some other geeks in the 1950s couldn't be bothered to write out the whole date when they invented computer programs. Instead of writing 1959, they got lazy and just wrote 59.

So come midnight Dec. 31, instead of saying 2000, the little clocks in our computers will reset to 00 – sending our electronic world back in time to 1900, and creating world-wide computer panic.

You don't believe it?

Weird things are happening already.

- In 1992, Mary B. of Winona, Minnesota was asked to register for kindergarten, because a computer mis-read her date of birth. It assumed that 88 meant **1988**. But Mary was actually 100 years older than her 4-year-old classmates.

- In 1997, a Dutch man was refused gas at a service station because his credit card had an expiry date of 00. The gas station computer decided the card was 97 years out of date – and had been issued 8 years before Henry Ford invented the Model-T.

- At Marks & Spencer, a tin of corned beef was rejected by a computer inventory system, which determined it had spoiled 97 years earlier – in 00. That's around the same time that Mary B., the world's oldest kindergarten student, was in grade 6.

All this is a small preview of what's supposed to happen when the Millennium bug comes to breakfast, on Jan. 1, 2000.

HOW WILL ANY OF THIS AFFECT ME?

If the geeks are right (and geeks are seldom wrong), come midnight Dec. 31:

- Your personal computer will think it's 1900, which means it's minus 100 years old, which is way before it was born or its warranty started – and that's enough to give anyone a mid-life crisis.

- Airline computers will see 00 and think it's 1900, which will supposedly make planes fall from the sky. "Ohmigod, I'm a supersonic jet and it's only 1900 and I haven't been invented yet so I guess I shouldn't be up here – I should be crashing to the *grrrrrroooooooun...*"

- Your brand new car won't start because its computer will think it's 1900, which is way before the invention of air bags, fuel injection, second gear, or – brakes! And even if your car works, your garage door won't open.

- If you manage to get to work you won't get in. Your office building's high-tech security system will think it's 1900, so no one is allowed into the building for another 100 years!

Harrop

January 2, 2000?

Murphy

DOES THIS MEAN IT'S CURTAINS 2000 FOR ME?

Before you write your will by hand, let's remember some other media-anticipated catastrophes that didn't come true. For instance:

- Nuclear waste will kill us (1965)

- Nuclear war will kill us (1968)

- The comet Kahoutek will hit Earth (1974)

- The energy crisis will send us back to the Stone Age (1978)

- Nuclear winter will kill us (1983)

- The depletion of the ozone layer will roast us (1985)

- The polar ice caps will melt, drowning us (1990)

- The Soviet Evil Empire will enslave the Earth (1960-1990)

JUST IN CASE, IS THERE ANYTHING WE CAN DO TO AVOID THE MILLENNIUM BUG?

The computer nerds say we have to hire them to rewrite all our computer programs – but these are the same people who used only two digits to write 1959 in the first place.

We have a better solution to the Millennium bug.

Forget it.

If the worst thing that can happen is that everything goes back to 1900, who cares?

Think of all the advantages of going back to 1900 and taking the century over again.

- There won't be much traffic. Henry Ford hasn't invented the automobile yet.

- You can buy lots of stocks. There should be twenty-nine years of a bull market.

- You'll be early for everything you do. ("Wanna go for a coffee? ... The movie doesn't start for another 100 years.")

- You'll be really young. "Hey, Susan, you don't look a day over minus forty."

- We'll have 59 years to make sure that next time round, we don't program our computers to have the Millennium bug.

- You'll be able to buy this book again...

MILLENNIUM MARKETPLACE

It's never too soon to protect yourself from the next Millennium.

Order now!

Millennium Bug Spray

Spray it on your computer or better yet spray it on anyone who mentions the Millennium bug.

Kills them dead.

Mb swatter also available.

Millennium Motel

Millennium pests check in, but they can't check out!

Free gift certificates available now.

The M-Chip

Blocks out all Millennium news, or other programming from your TV.

Protect your kids before the Millennium gets them.

A MILLENNIUM BUG SURVIVAL GUIDE

by Scott Feschuk

As the Millennium approaches, many people are bracing for chaos – no power, no phones, no junk mail, no transportation, no food, no cold beer.

Some Y2K survivalists are building fortified homes in the Arizona wilderness, buying generators, and stocking up on weapons, water and those Cadbury eggs you can only buy at Easter.

They may be crazy, but what if they're right? Just in case the post-1999 world proves more like Mad Max than Office Max, you *can* be ready – if you rip out this list of handy survival tips.

1. Be aware that airplanes can be an excellent source of food. Helpful tip: allow time for the wreckage to cool before searching for the snack cart.

2. Dead computers are excellent paperweights and beautiful, if potentially life-threatening, components for a baby's mobile.

3. Barbed wire makes for a secure perimeter and doubles as tinsel for the Christmas tree.

4. If you don't want to build your own hideout, find a quiet, deserted place, such as a Michael Bolton concert.

5. The guys on your doorstep wearing army fatigues and toting Uzi machine guns are not Amway salesmen, so don't invite them in – even if you're lonely. And anyway, how did they penetrate the razor wire?

6. An idea whose time is about to come: solar powered CD players.

7. Invest in a surface-to-air missile system that will still work – the catapult. Get a dependable security system, like the moat.

8. Convert all assets into canned tuna – the only safe haven.

9. Buy our recipe book – *100 Tasty Things You Can Do With A Fax Machine*.

10. On the bright side, you won't be bugged by that blinking 12:00 on your VCR anymore.

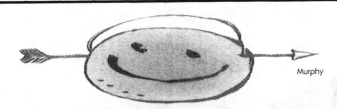

Murphy

THINGS WE HOPE GET HIT BY THE MILLENNIUM BUG

by Janet Torge

- The IRS
- Security gates, at private homes valued over $500,000
- Digital parking meters
- Digital bathroom scales
- Credit bureaus
- Car alarms
- Voice mail
- Muzak in stores
- Cell phones (except yours)
- General Pinochet's pace-maker
- The Golf Channel

The official shoe
of the Millennium...

Hughson

AIR *J*ESUS

Gable

5

Y1K

A brief history of the last 1000 years

We hear no end of hype about the approach of Y2K – the Year 2000. But how did they mark the first Millennium? Was there a lot of medieval hoopla? A Y1K bug? What was product placement like?

> *"Get your Millennium flagellation kit now: includes whips, flames and eye gouges."*

The facts have been covered up for a Millennium – until now. So let us take you back to...

THE STORY OF Y1K

by Mike Boone

Jaffé

995: THE BIG Y1K CHILL

As the first Millennium approached, every Christian who could read – eight clerics in Rome who played poker Wednesday nights – noticed that the book of Revelations contained some chilling warnings. Apart from cautioning that masturbation harmed eyesight, the book predicted that Satan would soon be loosed upon the world after serving a 1000-year term since the death of Christ.

Although his Judean lawyer had plea-bargained his charges down from felony villainy to misdemeanor malevolence, Satan had done a full Millennium of very hard time and was mightily pissed off as his release date approached.

The Bible predicted that a final battle between Good and Evil would take place at Armageddon (a large stadium in Constantinople, built in the hope of attracting a professional soccer franchise).

It also predicted that Good would triumph, after trailing Evil at the half. Following the game, the world as we know it would end and be replaced by a perfect new world: a heaven on earth, populated by the fair, the righteous, the strong and enough personal trainers and nannies to keep the aforementioned groups happy.

But then again, what if it Good didn't triumph? If Evil won, there would be hell to pay...

998: THE Y1K CRUSADES

In early 998, the Holy Roman Church developed the MAP (Millennium Action Plan) to help ensure the scenario ended well.

A special cadre of monks, trained to walk long distances while wearing sandwich boards, was sent to travel the Christian world warning: *The End is Near, Repent Before It's Too Late* and *For a Good Time in Rome, Call Pope Leo's Escort Service.*

A follow-up team worked the same territories two weeks later, selling fragments of the True Cross (which curiously resembled tongue depressors and were stamped "Union made in Lower Silesia").

Revenues from trinket sales swelled the papal coffers and were used to finance a Millennial crusade. Led by Richard, Cul de Cheval, everyone who had two serfs to rub together was invited to come recapture

Jerusalem from the Saracens, who had plans to turn it into an Islamic theme park.

The mission failed because Richard was cursed with a poor sense of direction and took a wrong turn in the Levant. Thus it came to pass that his army spent two years laying siege to a Club Med on the Red Sea. Fortunately, meals were included.

999: THE FIRST MILLENNIUM BUG

Fear swept the monasteries of Europe when monks became alarmed that illuminated manuscript materials, like nibs and ink, would crash at midnight, Dec. 31, 999. That meant falling to the ground, shattering and spraying monks' feet with bright, indelible ink.

Pope Innocente II was concerned that production of illuminated manuscripts would cease before publication of his *12 Steps to Millennial Bliss*, a self-help book for which he had been paid a high two-figure advance.

In his historic encyclical *Semper ubi Sub ubi*, Innocente (who had succeeded Pope Nolo Contendere IV in 986) advised monks to wear protective covering on their feet. An innovative monk, brother Georgio of Armenia took the Pope's instructions one step further. He invented a foot covering that used hex signs to ward off evil – and thus were born the argyle socks that bald men have worn with sandals for 1000 years.

1000: ENGLAND – MILLENNIUM EVE

Ethelred the Unready (son of William the Impotent and Helen the Frigid) acquired his nickname by delaying preparations for England's Millennium celebrations until late November, 999.

Because of Ethelred's poor planning, England was

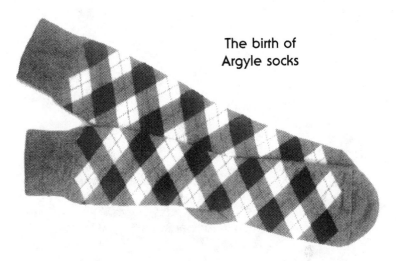

The birth of Argyle socks

unable to purchase balloons, fireworks or souvenir sportswear reading "My father went to liberate the Holy Lands from infidels, and all I got was this lousy hair shirt."

At the 11th hour of the 12th month, Ethelred made a desperate attempt to purchase confetti from Koleslaw of Poland, but the deal collapsed when the asking price – 1,500 virgins and Wales – was misinterpreted as 1,500 whales and a virgin. Anglo-Saxons were forced to usher in the first Millennium by drinking flat boar's blood and blowing up peasants. The result was an enduring national embarrassment over what British tabloids still call "The Great Millennial Cock-Up." Blowing up peasants is still a favorite pastime in parts of Northern Ireland.

1000 years later, this lack of preparedness still haunts England and many other countries. This has resulted in a determination to be ready when the clock strikes midnight on Dec. 31, 1999.

England has reportedly stored away fireworks, champagne, party hats and an emergency supply of peasants.

In the event of a Dec. 31, 1999 second coming, and a return match between Good and Evil, London bookmakers have Satan listed as a 4-1 favorite.

If the Devil wins, he is expected to demand a new deal worth 6 billion souls, with the standard 1000-year no-rematch clause.

The deal will be signed in blood.

JANUARY 1, 1001

Christians awaken to find their world has not been destroyed. They drink copious quantities of "hair of the boar," a celebratory hangover cure, before getting down to the business of drawing and quartering anyone who had predicted Millennial disaster.

Many Christians remain angry at the Church for trying to make a killing on salvation trinkets and Armageddon ready-to-wear. They contemplate converting to Judaism until they learn about circumcision, at which point most opt for less-demanding varieties of tree worship.

Faced with a crisis that imperils the Church's ability to last another 1000 years, Pope Mario III rekindles religious fervor by writing an early Latin version of *Miracle on 34th Street*.

Forgotten Headline Pages Through the Ages

"Some day all buildings will look like this":
Ramses II opens Pyramids

Two Commandments dropped: Now ten

33-Year-old carpenter walks on water

Great Wall construction hit by cost over-runs

"Plague Shmague," says doctor. "Take two leeches
and call me in the morning."

"Virginia Slims," Raleigh tells weight-conscious queen

Ludd-led walkout leaves looms idle

"Ivan turned terrible at two," says mom

Earth sucks, says Newton

Michelangelo lands big ceiling contract.
Estimates three coats

Tower in Pisa is fine, says architect

E=YK²
SURPRISING INVENTIONS OF THE LAST MILLENNIUM

by André Picard

Cummings

Everyone has heard of scientists whose discoveries changed the world, like Thomas Edison, who gave us the phonograph (now known as the compact disc player), and Jonas Salk, who created polio vaccine.

But there are many scientists who altered the course of history in ways they would never have imagined:

PHILLIPUS PARACELSUS

He was the first to treat disease with chemicals, giving birth to the pharmaceutical industry, the need for medicine cabinets in every house, litigation lawyers and the Grateful Dead.

BARTOLOMMEO CRISTOFORI

The Italian music lover invented the piano in 1709, forever condemning children to after-school piano lessons and elephants to slaughter for their ivory. His distant relative, Liberace, made the world wish Cristofori had also invented the sequin-remover.

JAMES PUCKLE

The British weapons buff invented the machine gun in 1718, paving the way for World War I, Bonnie and Clyde, and Star Wars. He always claimed the Puckle gun was designed for peaceful purposes.

LOUIS LENORMAND

Invented the parachute in 1783. It was not a big seller until the Wright Brothers managed to fly, 120 years later. But try to imagine a world without Evil Knievel, race cars, heli-skiing and space shuttles.

EDWIN BUDDING

Invented the lawn mower in 1831. This led to the creation of suburbs, countless amputations, noisy Saturday mornings and the expression "This Bud's for you."

FRIEDRICH MEISCHER

The German scientist discovered deoxyribonucleic acid (DNA) in 1869. But it didn't really matter until 1997, when O.J. Simpson proved that, mixed with blood, DNA makes gloves shrink.

MARIE CURIE

The Polish-French physicist won her first Nobel Prize for discovering radioactivity, which led to the bombing of Hiroshima, Chernobyl and Superman's x-ray vision. She never won a prize for another lasting contribution to humanity, the extra spicy shrimp curry.

ISAAC NEWTON

Formulated the laws of gravity (ensuring humans would never fly) and calculus (ensuring high school would never be pleasant). Hoping to save his reputation, the brainy Briton also invented the Prune Newton, which became a hit centuries later when someone with taste buds made an important ingredient change.

CLARENCE BIRDSEYE

In 1924, he invented frozen food, blessing the world with frozen peas and TV dinners. However, the stuff just piled up in freezers until decades later, when Percy Spencer invented the microwave.

ERIK ROTHEIM

The Norwegian inventor created the aerosol can, opening the door to earth-shattering products like whipped cream, Raid and spray-on hair. But his most enduring invention is the hole in the ozone layer.

JOSEPH BEGUN

The Polish scientist invented the tape recorder and the cassette, in 1934, creating the basic ingredients for rap music, Watergate and the Lewinsky tapes.

JAY C. HORMEL

A butcher looking for something to do with leftover parts of pigs, he gave the world Spam. The popular pink luncheon meat was the food of choice of Allied troops in World War II and may have saved the free world. It also inspired many artists, notably Monty Python, and the Internet sales revolution led by multi-level marketers (spammers).

BETTE NESMITH GRAHAM

Aislin

An executive secretary who invented Liquid Paper, because she could no longer correct her poor typing with an eraser after the advent of the electric typewriter. Graham eventually sold the company she created, for almost $50-million, and returned to the secretarial pool after investing it all in her next big idea, Liquid Chicken.

WHAT'S A THOUSAND YEARS?

by Willa Marcus

Amidst all the excitement, it's important to keep some perspective. So, say "Humbug!" to all those TV programs you'll be seeing about how much has changed in human history over the past 1000 years – and remember how little has really happened.

For Millennial relaxation, think *geologically.*

In the past 1000 years:

- North America and Europe have moved only 30 yards apart.

- Mount Everest has risen a scant 6 yards.

- The core of the Earth has cooled a mere 50 millionths of a degree.

- The crust of the ocean floor is 7.5 inches deeper.

- The Grand Canyon has gotten 2/10 of a yard deeper.

- The moon's surface hasn't changed at all, except for the addition of some astronaut footprints, a Land Rover and a golf ball.

- The Milky Way looked the same on January 1, 1000 as it will on January 1, 2000 and on January 1, 3000.

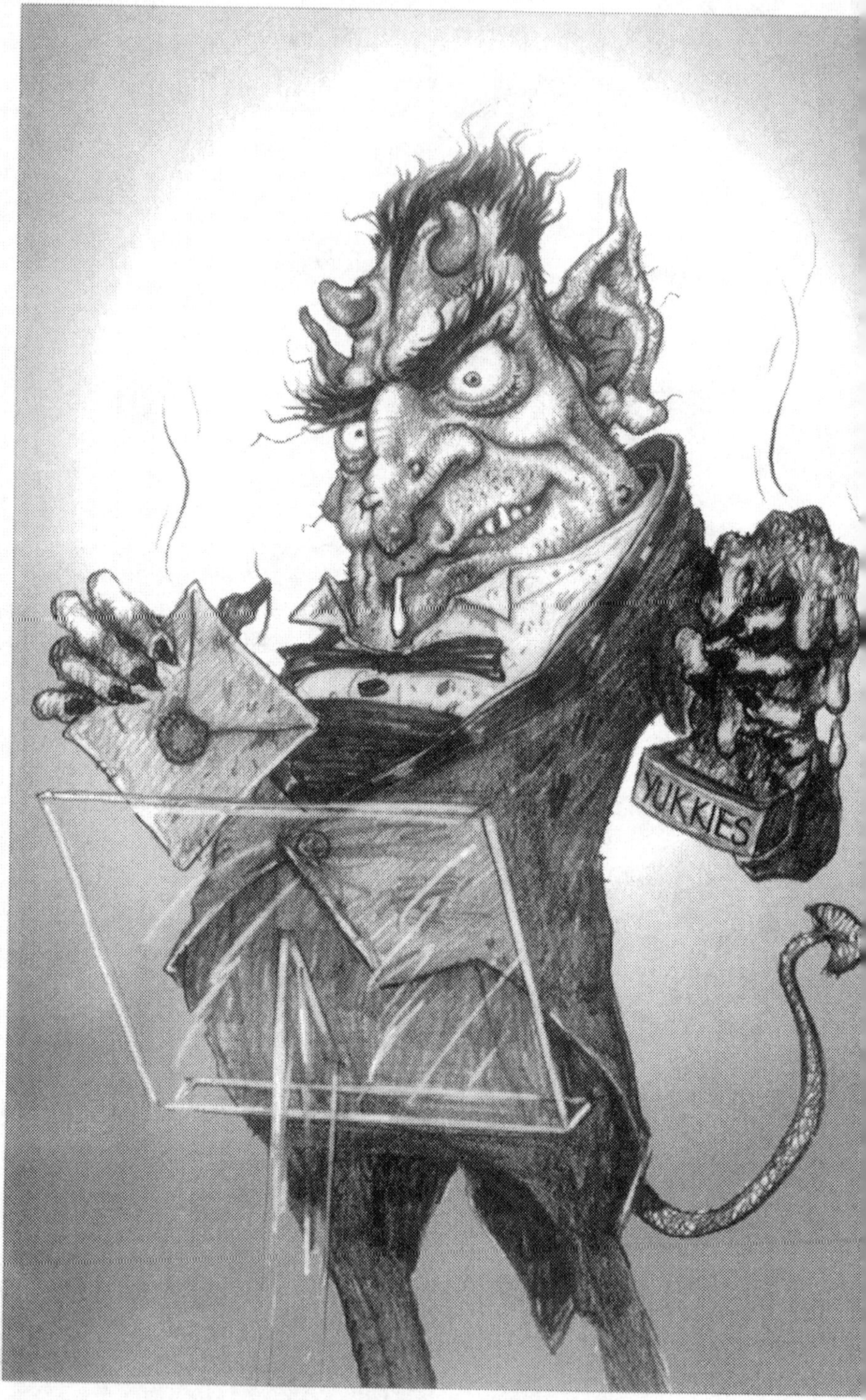
YUKKIES

Gable

THE YUKKIES

CHAPTER

4

Awards for 2000 years of bad books, bad songs, bad films & bad fashion

Entries have now officially closed for:

The Most Ludicrous Statement about the Millennium

TALKING MILLENNIALIST HEADS

Here are the nominees

Judge: Rick Salutin

NOMINEE 1:

"Because the cosmetics industry never tires in its quest to fulfill our needs almost before we are aware of them, its output now limns the footprint of apocalyptic dread... Our embrace of super soaps can *probably* be understood in light of a general foreboding that crystallizes around the new Millennium..."

New York Times Magazine,
May 1998

Congratulations to the authors for this splendid entry. When was the last time you read the word "limns"? Also, note the use of the word "probably". Why over-commit to the possibility? Perhaps some focus-groups could test it out...

NOMINEE 2:

"While the year 2000 has no obvious intrinsic significance, it readily lends itself to being imbued with extrinsic meaning, which is what makes it so mesmerizing... If the year 1000 C. E. is a reliable indicator, we will likely witness increasing frenzy as we approach the Millennial D-Day... Common sense can be expected to be submerged by a volcanic eruption of repressed subconscious matter... The Millennial threshold represents... an extraordinary opportunity for the creation of personal and collective meaning revisioning, and growth."

George Feuerstein
Parabola, spring 1998

A superb example of how you can spout any amount of pseudo-intellectual gibberish if you remember to say Millennium.

NOMINEE 3:

"In the 1990's there exists a pervasive sense of complacency, a turning toward immediate satisfactions, and an imaginative fatigue that is seemingly content with muddling through, barely taking more than a ritualistic notice of the Millennial shift that awaits us. "

Prof Richard Falk,

"The Paucity of the Millennial Moment"

from *"The Year 2000, Essays on the End"*

In other words, most of you just aren't imaginative enough to get worked up about this crock.

NOMINEE 4:

"Consider for example, these five innovations of the past thousand years: the state, the corporation, extensive crime organizations, religious pluralism, and the morally autonomous individual... Each was a noteworthy departure from its predecessor... The Millennium that was to come in A.D. 1000 uncovered challenges... that awaited the next ten centuries.... Inventing solutions to the problems they pose will provide enough challenges to occupy humanity for the next thousand years..."

John D. Montgomery, Harvard University,
World Policy Journal, summer 1998

It must be nice to think in thousand-year chunks, and make to-do lists for them as if you're getting ready for a weekend at the cottage.

NOMINEE 5:

"Millennial Fever is driving consumer behavior in all sorts of interesting ways, which means it offers marketing opportunities. But it won't last forever... the fever has a special intensity this time around, for several reasons. First, it's the turn of a Millennium, not just a century... as we get closer to the year 2000, the margin between end and beginning

becomes progressively narrower… don't present the
future as a brave new world, but the future as a new,
improved version of the present."

James R. Rosenfield,
American Demographics, December 1997

*Demographics, now the stupidest science,
meets the Millennium, the stupidest event.*

NOMINEE 6:

"When the President and I began to talk about how
as a country we could mark this turn of the calendar, you might guess that we came back to one
idea – what it meant to build a bridge to the 21st
century. When the President talked about the
bridge, he didn't mean, of course, a real bridge, but
he did mean one that would metaphorically be con-
structed by the gifts all Americans would give to
the future "

From a speech by First Lady Hillary Rodham Clinton.

*It depends on your definition of a "bridge." Or for
that matter, your definition of "a."*

NOMINEE 7:

Writer and Millennium author-philosopher Mark
Kingwell says ordinary people he meets plan to
ignore the Millennium and resist all the hoopla
around it. Kingwell responds to that in an interview
with the *Globe and Mail:* "I resist the resistance. I
don't want to fall into simply waving it all off… I
wanted to try to make
sense of my own compli-
cated feelings about this."

*Some of us just aren't sen-
sitive enough to have
complicated feelings about
the year 2000.*

Murphy

THE WORST SONGS OF THE MILLENNIUM

by Charles Gordon

Following are the top 20 of the 2000 worst songs of the Millennium. For aficionados, "McArthur Park" is number 34. "Itsy Bitsy Teeny Weenie Yellow Polka-Dot Bikini" is number 257. Songs 313 to 367 are by Neil Diamond.

1. **Deutschland Uber Alles**
2. **My Way** – Vegas Uber Alles
3. **Greensleeves** – A song written to commemorate the invention of the handkerchief.
4. **Memory** – by Andrew Lloyd Webber. Or anything else by Andrew Lloyd Webber.
5. **The Song of Solomon** – It's been in the Bible for what, 2000 years? Have you ever heard anybody sing it?
6. **Hey, Jude** – The Beatles classic contains the lyric Dah dah dah da-da-da dah, da-da-dadah.

7. **The Star Spangled Banner** – Now sung so slowly, it is expected to come to a dead stop just before Game 3 of the World Series.

8. **Na Na, Hey Hey, Kiss Him Goodbye** – This 1969 hit by Steam contains the lyric, Na-ha nah nah, na-na nah nah, hey, hey, good-bye, which is sung in hockey rinks. Also, it is clearly derivative of "Hey Jude".

9. **Do-Re-Mi** – The first line, "Doe, a deer, a female deer" signals a cruel attempt to force animals to sing scales.

10. **The Little Drummer Boy** – Some say "The Hawaiian Christmas Song" is the worst Christmas song ever. But "The Hawaiian Christmas Song" does not contain the expression "rump-pa-pum-pum."

11. **The Hawaiian Christmas Song**

12. **Lady of Spain** – The accordion was invented to play this song.

13. **Unfinished Symphony** – In any self-respecting educational institution, Schubert would get an incomplete.

14. **Auld Lang Syne** – After Dec. 31, 1999, this should never be sung again unless its lyrics are put into modern English – Old Lawn Sign.

15. **The Impossible Dream** – Proven by thousands of vocal versions – an Impossible Song.

16. **People** – Never, ever write a song about a magazine.

17. **100 Bottles of Beer on the Wall** – Believed to have caused an epidemic of alcoholism among school bus drivers.

18. **In the Year 2525** – A lame rock and roll re-working of the old song "In the Year 1525," in which Albert von Brandenburg became Duke of Prussia and Peru was divided between Huascar and Atahualpa, on the death of Huayna Capac. What was wrong with the original?

19. **(I Can't Get No) Satisfaction** – Should be (I Can't Get Any) Satisfaction.

20. **Smed Grbsaklv** – Old sentimental Mongolian drinking song about using a whole dead goat to sweep bloodstains off the floor of your yurt. The title translates literally as To Sir, With Love.

FASHION MISTAKES OF THE MILLENNIUM

by Joel Yanofsky

Ever since the first caveman and woman donned an out-of-season bearskin and loincloth, you know there was some style snob, a prehistoric Mr. Blackwell, shaking his head in dismay, grunting, "What were you thinking when you put that on?"

Fashion is fickle. So is history. Just glance at an old photo some time: the bell bottoms, the tie-dye T-shirt, the micro-mini-skirt, and you'll find yourself asking a familiar question, "What was I thinking?"

THE WORST-DRESSED PEOPLE OF THE LAST 1000 YEARS...

JOAN OF ARC

You must have been hearing voices to wear a simple burlap shift to your own auto-da-fé. And on your last public appearance – to die! Perhaps the layered look would have been a more practical and, dare we say, hotter outfit? Something bright, in natural fibers – preferably asbestos? No matter, Joan, darling, you'll still go down in history as the first woman to utter the now all-too familiar complaint: *"But I'm only going to wear this once."*

Bado

ERIK, THE RED

Black, Erik, black! Even an uncouth Viking should know that whether you are off exploring Greenland or just raping and pillaging a neighboring village, nothing says cutthroat like basic black. And nothing goes better with those always difficult to mix-and-match bloodstained accessories.

Bado

SIR LANCELOT

We're sorry, but we just don't see the appeal of a suit of armor. Yes, it wrinkles less than linen, but chain mail just doesn't, how shall we put it, breathe. Besides, you can never wear it in the rain without squeaking. Chivalry isn't dead, Lance, it's just a little rusty. Because if you think King Arthur isn't going to hear you clanging into Guinevere's boudoir in the wee hours, you're even more in the dark ages than a knight ought to be.

Bado

ST. FRANCIS OF ASSISI

Bado

We know it gets cold and damp in a 13th century monastery, but white socks and sandals with a brown robe? Oh brother, Brother! If you hadn't been so busy communing with the birds, you might have realized that the only reason none of the other monks mentioned your fashion *faux pas* was that they'd taken a vow of silence. Take it on faith, they went through hell to keep their mouths shut.

ELIZABETH I, THE VIRGIN QUEEN

You're a queen, you're a redhead, you're a powerful working woman. You could have had it all. But with all that pomp and circumstance and those high ruffled necks – no love bites for you – it's no wonder you died, as your court would have tastefully put it, "intact."

JOHN KEATS

TB or not TB, that is the question. The Kate Moss of your time, you milked the consumptive waif look for all it was worth. But do us a favor – lose the tights, the puffy shirt and take that hanky out of your sleeve. A thing of beauty is a joy forever – but maybe not.

FLORENCE NIGHTINGALE

We love a gal in uniform. We'll even admit that the stiff, starchy look made the Crimean War a blast for a while. But Flo, that silly bonnet and cape weren't exactly a morale booster for the boys on the frontlines. You know what the talk around the field hospital was, don't you?: The Lady of the Lamp gets dressed in the dark.

Bado

ALBERT EINSTEIN

The laws of physics may be relative, but bad hair is always bad hair. If you were so smart, how come you couldn't invent Brylcreem? Eh, wise guy? And you call yourself a genius. Vidal Sassoon, now that's our idea of a genius.

ELVIS PRESLEY

Whoever squeezed a thicker you into a tighter and tighter sequined white jump suit should be brought up on manslaughter charges. If someone had just visited a Memphis Portly Men's Shop and bought a XL pullover and some stretchy Big Man slacks, the King would still be alive today.

Murphy

ELIZABETH II

Lose the drab suits, the fifties hairstyle and the handbag. What have you got in there anyway? Your bus pass?

Cummings

THE WORST MOVIES OF THE MILLENNIUM

by Jay Stone

The history of motion pictures can be divided roughly into two eras: a) the dawn of time until the actual invention of motion pictures, and b) the real part.

The earliest age involved running quickly past cave drawings with your eyes squinched up, blinking at 24 frames a second. Works from this pre-motion picture age, such as the "original" Jurassic Park, the dimly-lit musical *New Faces of 68 B.C.*, and *The Four Commandments* – a quickie documentary – are now all but forgotten. It wasn't until 1895, at the Cinematographe Lumière in Paris, that movies were projected and mankind could finally bask in the dream-like glow of the "magic lantern" and complain that the only reason they made the truffles so salty was to sell more champagne.

And so, we tip our hats to those hardy pioneers with their oil-fired lanterns and their swell new way of meeting chorus girls and proudly present the 25 worst movies of the Millennium:

The 19th Century

1. *Woman Running*
2. *The Arrival of a Train At The Station*
3. *Antoine's Naughty Hand Shadows*
4. *The Arrival of a Train At The Station Meets Woman Running*
5. *A Very Lumière Christmas*

The worst movies ever!

2000 THUMBS DOWN

Bado

The 20th Century

    6. *The Rowboat Potemkin*: A rare early failure by Eisenstein.

    7. *The Jazz Singer*: "You ain't heard nothing yet," turned out to be a warning.

    8. *God's Stepchildren*: An actress shakes her head and declares, "No... *emphatically*... no." Belatedly, we realize she is actually reading the script's stage directions into her lines. (Courtesy of J. Hoberman)

    9. *Terror of Tiny Town*: The first, and still worst, all-midget western.

10. *Rocky III*: Yo, Adrian. I'm a bum again.

11. *Rambo*: First Blood II: Yo, Viet Cong. I'm a soldier again.

12. Everything with a II after the title except *The Godfather*.

13. *The Island of Dr. Moreau*: Marlon Brando with an ice bucket on his head.

14. *Blue*: God-awful film starring Terence Stamp with only one redeeming line: "I'm tired... especially of you."

15. *Barb Wire*: Pamela Anderson rescues post-apocalyptic America from fascism and undersized bosoms.

16. *The Postman*: Kevin Costner rescues post-apocalyptic America from fascism and shoddy mail service.

17. *Howard the Duck*: The first, and still worst, of the waterfowl sex-and-murder romps.

18. *I Spit On Your Grave*: Oh yeah? Well, I spit on yours.

19. *Sorority Babes in the Slimeball Bowl-O-Rama*: Well, how good can it be?

20. *On Deadly Ground*: Stephen Seagal saves the Arctic, then gives a lecture about the dangers of non-renewable sources of energy, and still doesn't change his expression.

21. *Peyton Place*: It was just a small New England town, but under the respectable facade bubbled desire, lust, and Lana Turner's acting.

22. *The Bonfire of the Vanities*: And me without marshmallows.

23. *Revenge of the Teenage Vixens From Outer Space*

24. *Revenge of Antoine's Naughty Hand Shadows*

25. *Revenge of the Lumière Brothers*

THE WORST INVENTIONS OF THE LAST 2000 YEARS

- Dinner theater
- Guillotine
- Bagpipes
- Hair in a can
- One man seesaw
- Seadoo
- Speedo
- PCBs
- Cool Whip
- False eyelashes
- Cheese Whiz
- Girdles
- Suit of armor
- Polyester pant suits
- Snuff
- Cummerbunds
- Chewing tobacco
- Bow ties
- Mood rings
- Black velvet paintings
- Psychoanalysis
- Popcorn topping at movies
- Telemarketing
- Cigarettes

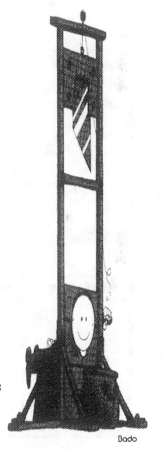

Bado

THE WORST MANUSCRIPTS OF THE MILLENNIUM

by Richard King and Jon Kalina

There is no shortage of candidates for the worst books of the last two thousand years. The printing press wasn't invented until well into the second Millennium, but this did not deter people from writing truly awful books in manuscript form.

Following are the worst unpublished manuscripts of all time.

Murphy

THE UNEXPURGATED LEVITICUS: You thought the final version in the Bible was slow-moving, you should have seen the first draft. There were 700 Kosher laws. Apparently by the same authors as **GENESIS, EXODUS** and **DEUTERONOMY**, although many think they should have stopped at a trilogy.

ODYSSEY 2: ULYSSES' RESTLESS HOURS: Back at home, Ulysses tires of taking out the garbage. Takes up lawn bowling. Doesn't like it. Takes up slaughtering. Likes it.

LIEF ERICSON'S NORSE/BEOTHUK TRAVELERS' DICTIONARY Also by the same author: **THE TWO BEST RESTAURANTS IN ICELAND** and **86 WAYS TO SAY "COD."**

GHENGIS KHAN'S EQUESTRIAN MANUAL AND CAMPING GUIDE FOR THE LONELY LOOTER.

Before Dante gets into his stride he writes a forgettable how-to manual for Renaissance humour writers, called **THE SITUATION COMEDY.**

Boccaccio's first effort, **THE PENTAGON**, is rejected by a 14th-century publisher, whose rejection note says "too short and not dirty enough."

Chaucer's early draft of **THE MILLER'S TALE**, starts with one of the most famous lines in English Literature: "Englande swinges like a pendulum dost."

In 1453 Gutenberg invents moveable type and prints his first book, **THE BIBLE IN PIG LATIN**. However, most critics still consider **EVITICUS-LAY** to be unreadable.

Before he gets the Reformation under way, Martin Luther produces an early draft known as **NINETY-FIVE EASY THESES**.

In the 16th century, Shakespeare writes his only unpublished play, a story about a traveling salesman, set in the 1500s, entitled: **JULIET DOES THE MERCHANT OF VENICE.**

In 1667 John Milton publishes the first volume of his Paradise Trilogy, followed by the other two unpublished works: **PARADISE STILL MISSING** and **PARADISE FOUND**.

In 1726, after an in-camera trial so secret that even he could not attend, Voltaire flees to England where he writes his scathing satire of the Enlightenment, **CANDIDE CAMERA.**

In 1730 the play, **I MARRIED A TEENAGE LEVITICUS**, opens. Closes same night.

Tobias Smollett writes a guide to London delis: **THE ADVENTURES OF PEREGRINE PICKLE**. He is furious when he is upstaged by another deli-owner who writes **THE SCARLET PUMPERNICKEL**.

Catherine the Great becomes Czarina of Russia in 1762 and writes an unpublished novel whose title is stolen two centuries later: **THE HORSE WHISPERER**.

Americans start to write. Three years before the Alamo, Davy Crockett publishes his **AUTOBIOGRAPHY OF A HAT** which becomes an underground classic. A year later Jim Bowie writes his rip-off **AUTOBIOGRAPHY OF A KNIFE,** which bombs.

Americans invent the sequel. James Fenimore Cooper begins with **MOHICANS I: THE WILDERNESS SAGA** and ends with **MOHICANS XVII: WHAT'S A MOHICAN?** The last volume becomes known as **FINALLY, THE LAST OF THE MOHICANS.**

The French Revolution spurs many famous terrible manuscripts, such as Marie Antoinette's cookbook, **LIVING ON CAKE** and Robespierre's poignant broadside, **IF THEY CAN'T TAKE A JOKE, OFF WITH THEIR HEADS.**

In France, Mme. Gustave Flaubert writes a first draft about the ambivalence of gender, called **MY DAMN OVARIES.**

Victor Hugo writes the novel that is considered his best work, **MISERY**, followed by his unpublished **MISERY LOVES COMPANY**.

Nathaniel Hawthorne completes his unpublished series, **A IS FOR ADULTERY, B IS FOR BAD GIRL, C IS FOR COQUETTE**,... ending with **Z IS FOR ZIS HAS GONE ON LONG ENOUGH.**

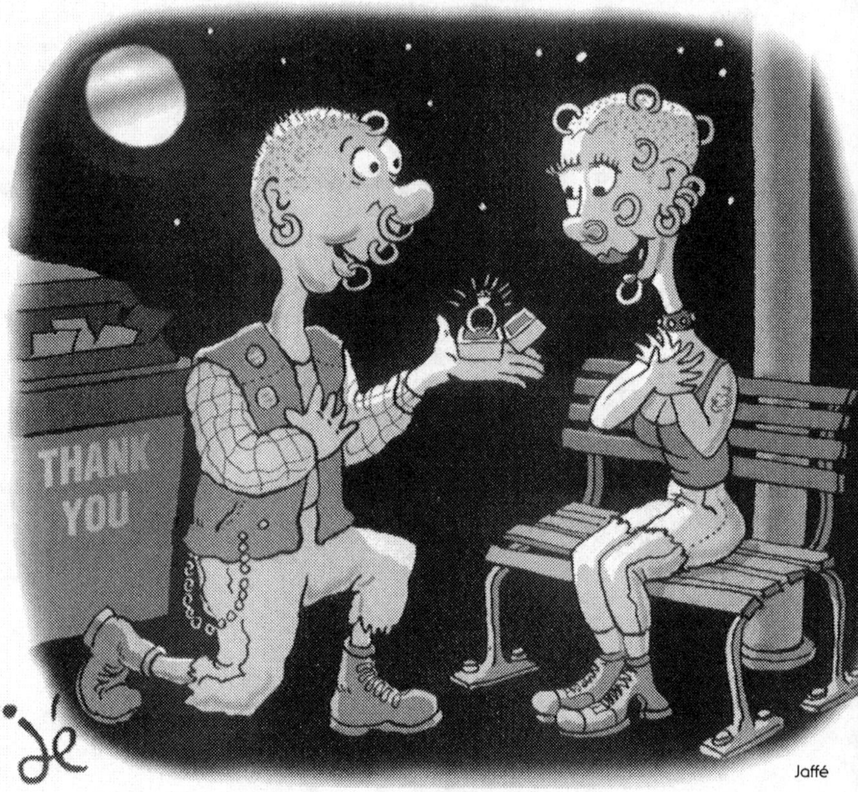
THANK YOU

Jaffé

Gable

I'M OK, YOU'RE 2K

Trends to watch out for in the next 10 centuries

Here's a peek at the latest millitrends – from millipedes and millifeuilles, to milliskirts and millisex.

Y wait a millisecond? Be the first on your planet to be forewarned about what you'll face in the next Millennium.

SEX...

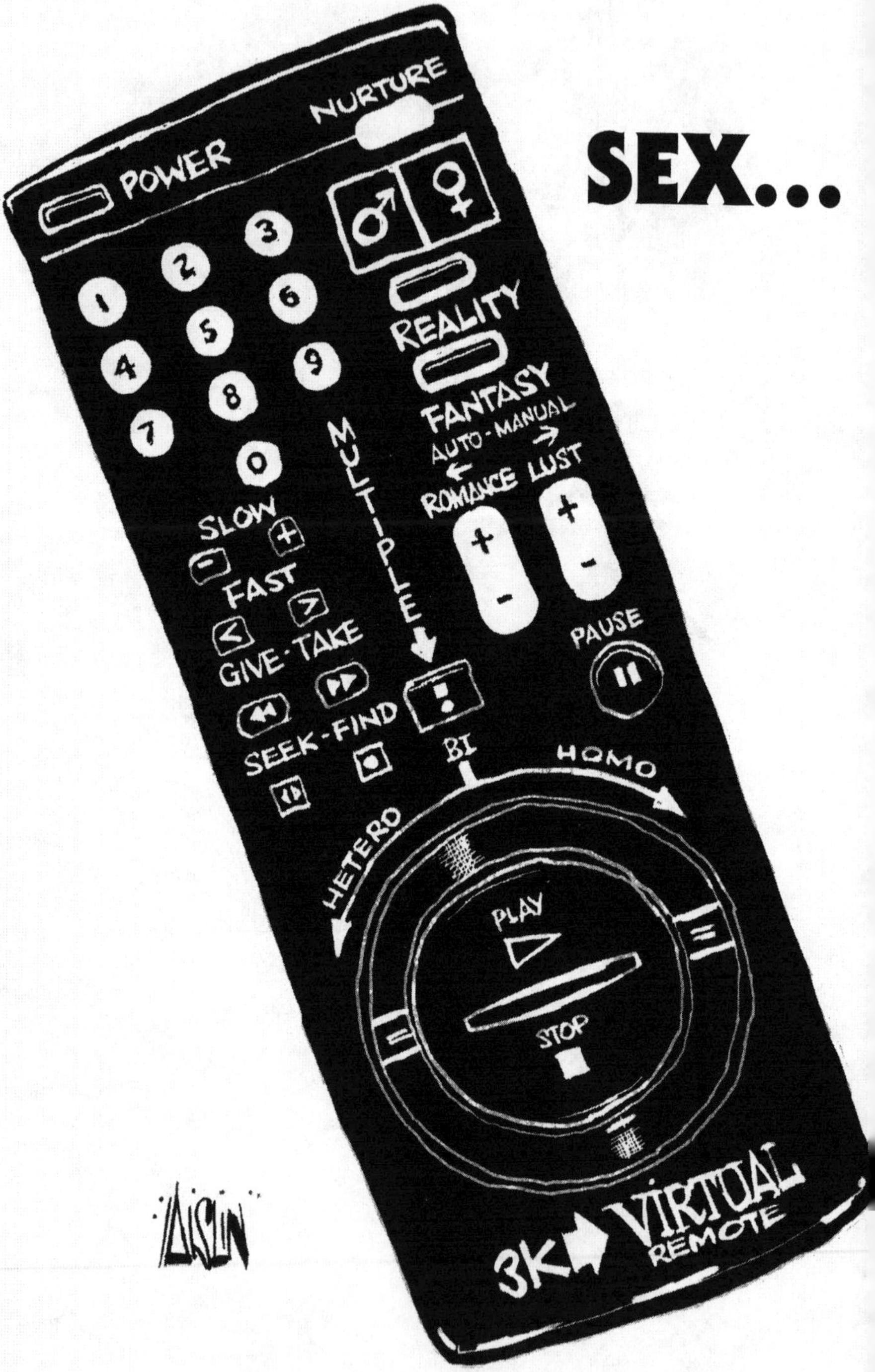
NURTURE
POWER
1 2 3 4 5 6 7 8 9 0
REALITY
FANTASY
AUTO-MANUAL
ROMANCE LUST
MULTIPLE
SLOW
FAST
GIVE-TAKE
SEEK-FIND
PAUSE
BI
HOMO
HETERO
PLAY
STOP
3K VIRTUAL REMOTE
AISLIN

...AND HOW TO GET SCREWED BEFORE THE END OF THE MILLENNIUM

by Josey Vogels

Remember when sex was just sex? It used to be that all it took to get under the covers was a cheap bottle of wine, a bed and maybe some nice clean underwear.

But plain old sex doesn't cut it as we head into the next Millennium. Now, we need bells, whistles and whips. Why settle for plain old boring sex when there are so many promises of something new, improved – and preferably fat-free?

Sex at the dawn of the Millennium will be something like this:

> "He gently caressed her saline-packed breasts and liposucted thighs, while cooing over her full collagen-injected lips, and porcelain-like botax-pumped skin. She reached down to feel the Viagra-induced hardness of his cosmetically enlarged penis and ran her hands over his freshly-shaved, surgically pumped pecs. He sipped from his cup of Yohimbe tea while they enjoyed a dinner of oysters to get them randy. She slipped in the "Beyond The Kama Sutra" video, he read her passages from the best-selling 24-hour Orgasm. Then they slathered each other with lavender oil and made tantric love for hours under the glowing light of the eternity candles."

SEX TRENDS WE'LL SEE IN THE NEW MILLENNIUM

- Drive-through bawdy houses.
- Virtual condoms.
- With global warming and world flooding, water-proof vibrators will become very popular.
- Blow jobs will be considered an act of Congress.
- A third gender – combining men's inability to communicate and women's hyper-sensitivity. S/he sits silently on the bar stool, watching the ball game and weeping inconsolably during the car ads.
- As same-sex relationships grow, there will be a best-selling book called *Men are from Mars and Men are from Mars*.

TECHNOLOGY

- New computer software will allow you to videotape yourself having sex in your dreams.
- Sex in outer space: Anti-gravity will become the latest cure for impotency. Despite enhanced flexibility and positioning, most people will continue to use the missionary position while orbiting Mars.
- When the Y2K bug hits, all internet sex will return to Victorian morals and practises. The most popular web site, *www.rubens.com,* will feature paintings of hefty Parisienne courtesans in whale-bone corsets. The big radio show will be a sex advice phone-in called "Ask Edward VII."

Aislin

NEW DRUGS BY THE MAKERS OF VIAGRA

- **Directra** – A dose of this drug, given to men before they take car trips, caused 72 per cent of them to stop and ask directions.

- **Complimentra** – In clinical trials, 82 per cent of men noticed when their girlfriends got a new haircut. Currently being tested to see if the effects extend to noticing new clothing.

- **Afteragra** – Post-coital wakeup pills for men.

- **Daddyagra** – Men taking this drug report a sudden, overwhelming urge to change diapers and wash out the bathtub.

- **Niagara** – Perfect for the Second Coming.

- **Buyagra** – Gets men to like shopping.

- **Sighagra** – Makes guys more sensitive.

- **Guyagra** – All purpose.

- **Male birth control** (*no, really they've almost got it*).

Aislin

OTHER TRENDS

Privacy will disappear and the "tell-all" principle will rule public discourse. Why chat to your corner grocer about the weather when you can make small talk about your sex life:

"Anything new?"

"Not much. My husband spanked me – and you?"

"Nah, the usual missionary stuff.
I can't get my husband to try anything."

"Then try the croissants –
they're fresh this morning."

SEX WILL BE GOVERNMENT-REGULATED, LIKE EVERYTHING ELSE

Orgasms for women will be mandatory in each sexual encounter. Failing to provide one during three consecutive sexual encounters will result in a fine of $50. Other fines will include:

- Falling short of the mandatory 20 minutes of foreplay – $25.
- Refusing to try a new position – $75.
- Commenting on penis size – $100.

Census forms will include a question about your sexual preferences and practices:

- How many people in your household enjoy S&M or light bondage?
- Number of sexual enhancement devices in your household?
- Which fetishes are represented in your household?

The G-Spot will be declared an official landmark, with guided tours available for a small fee, while the clitoris will be moved to a new and more convenient location.

FIRST FACE IN SPACE!

by Allen Abel

Chapleau

In 1962, Marine hero and test pilot John Glenn orbited the Earth three times, alone. In 1998, Democratic Senator John Glenn orbited the Earth 140 times accompanied by six astronauts, two toadfish, some house plants and a crate of cockroaches.

It was a reminder that space was becoming a busy place.

The interplanetary vacuum had been rather lonely before Glenn's first flight: only two brave Soviet fliers, two fearless American jetjockeys, a Communist dog named Leica and a Republican chimpanzee named Ham had preceded him.

But now that a 77-year-old politician has been successfully lifted off the planet (and, alas, allowed to come back down), the possibilities for expanding the zero-gravity population are endless.

Dozens of respectable engineering companies and lunatic dreamers are moving ahead with plans for reusable (they hope) civilian spacecraft. They plan to make orbital cruising affordable to anyone with $98,000 to blow on a 15-minute trip and the limited intelligence to climb aboard what astronaut Wally Schirra called, "an explosive rocket made of four million parts, all of them supplied by the lowest bidder."

Meanwhile, Russia's space program has fallen on such hard times that its cosmo-commissars plan to launch a worldwide sweepstakes for a civilian to win a nine-day holiday in space.

"It is the ultimate competition for the end of the Millennium," said an official with EMCI Marketing, which is handling the deal between Russia and an unnamed U.S. multinational. "It will put a civilian on Mir within 24 months." (Second prize is rumored to be 9 days at the Club Med in Kosovo).

The new Millennium will finally answer humanity's age-old dream and bring outer space within the reach of ordinary citizens. Voyagers will be able to strap themselves in, hear the countdown, feel the giant engine's rumble and soar into the vast, empty blackness.

Then, after floating around for a minute or two, vomiting profusely, and plummeting back to earth, they will tote their big helmet bags back to their earthly domiciles as members of a new tribe of astro-humans.

"I am home from the heavens," they will proudly announce.

"Don't give me that crap," their wives will say. "You've been bowling again."

Aislin

WHO WILL THESE INTREPID ADVENTURERS BE?

The first decades of the new Millennium are certain to witness:

- The First Marriage in space

- The First Divorce Settlement in space

- The First TV Sitcom shot in space

- The First Texas Cage Tag-Team Wrestling Death Match in space

- The First Governor of Minnesota in space (see above)

- The First 100-Yard Dash in space

- The First Athlete Caught Using Drugs in space

- The First Squeegee Kid in space

- The First Punching Out of a Squeegee Kid in space

- The First Dentist To Do Root Canal Work in space

- The First Old Woman Left To Die In Her Own Excrement Surrounded By 73 Cats Despite Having Four Grown Children In The Same Capsule in space

Y2KULTURE

by Suanne Kelman

It's hard to believe that only 1000 years ago, culture was barely more than a four-letter word.

You had your medieval monks turning out illuminated manuscripts, you had your bawdy folk songs about the virgin birth, and that was pretty well that.

But culture has come out of the cloisters in recent centuries, thanks to the printing press, the recording industry and television. As the new Millennium approaches, we stand at the very summit of human civiliza-

Culture then...

Gable

tion, enriched by the cultural wealth of Marilyn Manson, Jerry Springer and the *Sports Illustrated* Swimsuit Edition.

Sadly, there is nowhere to go but down. Here's what you'll be missing on the cultural scene in the next 1000 years.

THE NEO-NEO-CLASSICAL ERA

Over the next few centuries, human beings will forget the purpose of books, since they don't fit into even the oldest VCRs. However, they will continue to be enriched by the masterpieces of the Heavy Ages via the internet.

These Web Classics may have to compress details a bit.

By 2487 A.D., **Romeo and Juliet** will read more economically: *"The Montagues think the Capulets* *suck and the feelings are, like, mutual. The boy meets the girl, and the girl freaks out and pretends to kill herself, okay? Then the boy, like, really kills himself, the girl really kills herself, and their parents feel just awful, you know?"*

Moby Dick will also be far more accessible in the Web Classics edition: *"Man fights whale. Whale wins."*

The gradual death of words will be more than made up for by adding pictures and music. The breakthrough will come in the very near future, in the form of The Spice Girls' soul-searching music video **Anna Karenina** with Baby Spice surprising the critics with her maturity in the title role.

Other musicians will follow suit, with unexpected results:

The Adventures of Tom Sawyer will become a short but sizzling hip hop dance show called *Paint Da Fence*, the first in a long series of wildly successful literary adaptions by Mississippi rap artist No Sweat.

Culture now...

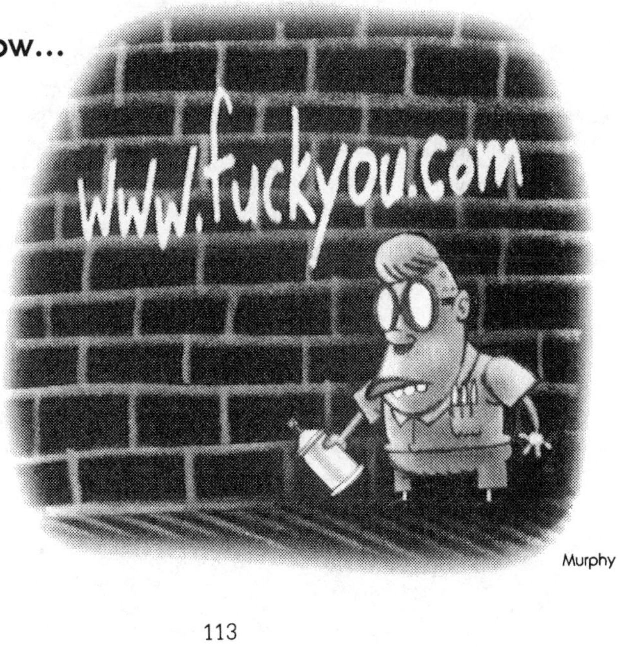
www.fuckyou.com
Murphy

Ulysses will be transformed into Boom-Boom-Bloom by U2; and Tolstoy will inspire a video classic: **"War – Huh! and Peace – What are They Good for? Absolutely nothing!"**

Bill Gates will eventually revive the Classic Comics Illustrated concept, this time with virtual images.

Russkie.sony@microsoft will make a fortune with **Crime and Punishment Lite** featuring Leonardo DiCaprio as Raskolnikov and Jerry Seinfeld as the pawnbroker.

THE RENAISSANCE REPLAYED

Last time round, we rediscovered the ancient classics. This time round, we will repackage the later classics, even as the originals crumble into dust from pollution.

The masterpieces of **Rembrandt** and **Van Gogh** will be marketed as screen-savers. The Franklin Mint will do a roaring business in **Sistine Chapel** wallpaper.

Like **Shakespeare** dramatizing the death of Julius Caesar, artists of the next Millennium will plunder history for inspiration. The great classics of our own times – like "Three's Company," and "The Dick Van Dyke Show" will be re-interpreted again and again, though few works will match the artistic grandeur of the Merchant-Ivory series known as the **"Hawaii 5-0 Quartet."**

Our own Millennium's most exalted art form – the sitcom – will survive well into the 26th century, its profound stories and characters feeding the planet's myriad talk shows.

The descendants of **Oprah Winfrey** will interview computer-gene recreations of the casts of "I Love Lucy," "The Brady Bunch" and "My Mother the Car."

Caring hosts will urge **Ozzie and Harriet** to explore the dark side of their relationship. The **Lone Ranger and Tonto** will sob uncontrollably while revealing – eight centuries too late – their true feelings for each other, and their horses.

Students of the future will study the texts of sitcoms, with exam questions like:

"Explain the stagecraft in: Int: **Jerry's** apartment. **Kramer** enters."

"What exactly did **Ralph Kramden** mean by 'To the moon, Alice!'? Please relate to Neil Armstrong's 'one small step.'"

There will be PhD theses on "the use of metaphor in **Dharma & Greg**" and "The influence of the Kabala on **The X-files**."

THE RETURN OF THE MIDDLE AGES (OR A TIME SO LITE IT'S DARK)

When humanity seeks spirituality and meaning, it will turn to the most uplifting art of the next 1000 years – fashion.

Clothing will nudge old statues and paintings from museums, as the cultured strive to polish their understanding of the maxi, the blazer, the teddy and the cross-trainer.

The effete and over-educated may still recognize names like Chaucer, Goethe, Beethoven and Eddie Murphy. But reverence will be reserved only for true genius: Armani, Ralph Lauren, Donna Karan and the God called Tommy.

In the enlightened age to come, believers will kneel to pray at the shrines of Versace the Martyr – the Saint Sebastian of the new Millennium. These holy places will be conveniently located in all ancient malls, and in the lobby-churches of Our Lady Diana of the Sorrows, where candles can be lit for souls of those maimed by land mines or dressed by Wal-Mart.

The Millennial Pet

by André Picard

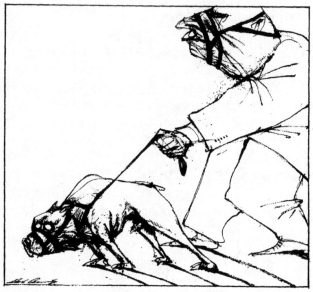

Cummings

For centuries now, we have had the same old boring pets.

With the arrival of the 21st century, however, it's time to admit that cats will never be friendly and rarely catch mice. Their principal contribution to humanity has been to boost the profits of pharmaceutical companies that sell anti-histamines.

As for dogs, they drool and remain incontinent their entire lives. And they hump your leg.

Some best friend.

It's time for a pet that will stand the test of time, a pal who'll remain loyal and hip for the next thousand years. What more fitting choice than the millipede?

Millipedes are often dismissed as small, harmless, insignificant creatures. But that's just pet food industry propaganda. They may be spineless, but they are colorful – usually red and green (the ideal

116

Murphy

Christmas gift). Millipedes can also do party tricks, like curling up into a ball and springing forward. They eat kitchen scraps, they don't get urinary tract infections and they don't have to be spayed or neutered. When you head out for the weekend, there are no kennel fees.

Millipedes are blind, but they "see" by tapping their antennae on the ground, meaning they have rhythm. Best of all, some species glow in the dark.

All in all, millipedes are the perfect Millennial pets for a number of reasons:

1. No need for a pooper scooper or litter box.

2. If they break a leg or two, so what?

3. They're non-allergenic.

4. They don't make hideous noises
   when they're in heat.

5. They give great hugs.

6. You don't have to walk them.

7. They don't chase cars.

8. They won't bite the mailman.

9. They're better dressed than ants.

10. They can kick a centipede's ass.

DESIGNER GENES

by Jon Kalina and Stephen Orlov

Scientific pundits are now predicting a brand new-Millennium product that may enhance your family's lifestyle – children from Designer Genes. If the experts are right, programming your own human embryos will become as commonplace as designing your own kitchen. "I'll have a violin prodigy in a pale off-white shade with a slight Scandinavian accent and a high IQ."

IN VITRO FERTILIZATION

Murphy

And why not? You want choice and you should have it. Already you let Giorgio design your suits and sunglasses, Ralph your blazers and bed sheets and Victoria your lingerie and facial creams. Why not trust them with your kids? Don't designer children deserve designers too?

It's time to go on-line and net shop for a DNA mix that's just right for you. Choose from these sample lines:

THE ARMANI COLLECTION

Pricey, but doesn't your family deserve the best? The Armani collection features children with no waist line and pleat-compatible thighs. Also features broad shoulders that come with Magic Grip™ that "magically" holds a draped jacket. How about a muscular, hairless chest that's insulated and ideal for loose unbuttoned shirts, even on ice cold days? Or teal-blue eyes that see in the dark even when sporting black-mirrored sunglasses?

THE POLO LINE

Ralph's team can offer you several models to choose from. Consider the popular preppy look -- comes with genes for thick straight hair, strong chins and no allergies to wool or cotton. Durable. Another popular choice: faux cowboy/girl child. Comes with feet that fit cowboy boots and eyes that squint at the distant horizon.

THE VICTORIA SECRET BOUDOIR

Your own made-to-measure Barbie daughter. Victoria's secret genes come in a choice of small, x-small, Anor-X-ic or Anor-XX-ic™. Order long lanky legs for silk stockings, knob-free knees for mini-skirts. And don't forget those Wondr-Breasts™, sure to fit strapless, padless bras and ideal for V-neck sweaters. Your choice of six cleavages. Streamlined TinyFeet™ fit elegantly into high stiletto heels. Built-in stabilizers make for perfect balance even while running down a flight of stairs!

THE L.L. BEAN CROWD

Want a child that fits in with your active outdoor life-style? Mix and match from the L.L. Bean unisex line, offered in Hiker, Skier or Mountain Man/Woman. Comes with backpack-ready shoulders, Kodiak Feet that never wrinkle when wet, and Thinsulate skin. WindChill™ earlobes, Nordic Fleece hair and optional Turtle Neck™ make this child a perfect companion for a Himalayan trek or just a brisk walk in the woods.

THE TIMBERLAND WATERPROOF CHILD

Kids that travel well in any climate. Sleep in any bed. Eat all cuisines. No jet lag. Look as fresh when they get off the plane as when they left home.

THE ROCK 'N' ROLL MILLENNIUM

by Mark Lepage

Chapleau

My my, hey hey, Rock 'n' Roll is here to stay — for a thousand more years, or until every possible commercial opportunity has been explored, whichever comes first. Here are some of the events the publicists have planned, so far:

- January 8, 2000: To mark the 65th anniversary of his birth, Elvis makes simultaneous appearances – at selected Wal-Marts.

- The Rolling Stones Steel Wheelchairs tour. Expect stiff competition from The Who's Quadriplegia. The Zombies also get in on the act, with the first posthumous rock concert.

- Thirty years in the planning, the surviving Beatles reunite. The same night, the killers of John Lennon, Brian Jones, Biggie Smalls and Tupac Shakur form a band and stage a live internet concert. Sirhan Sirhan and Charles Manson buy the rights.

- Prince, who once changed his name to an unpronounceable glyph, becomes an unpronounceable concept without bodily form. His wife sues for divorce, claiming he's never there for her.

- Madonna, unable to find a suitable lover, clones herself. The couple splits, citing irreconcilable differences.

- Accusing the rest of the pop world of sampling/expropriating his rhythm tracks for the past 20 years, James Brown sues everybody who is not James Brown.

- The grave of Milli Vanilli suicide Rob Pilatus is found to be empty. So they throw the other one in there.

- Satan makes a surprise appearance at the annual Beggars' Banquet fundraising dinner, planning to call in Keith Richards' loans. Richards kicks Satan's ass.

- The 505th posthumous Hendrix album is released, making him the first artist ever to release 100 times more records dead than alive.

- Puff Daddy is critically wounded in a drive-by shooting. The enterprising rapper sets his ECG beeps to breakbeats and sells 27 million copies of his album, *Flatline*.

- *Manilow: The Musical* becomes the first Broadway show in history not to sell a single ticket.

- The Fat Lady. She sings. Loud.

Beyond Vegetarianism

by Alan Mendelsohn and Willa Marcus

In the next Millennium, the trend toward considering the feelings of all living things will continue to spread. Vegetarianism will move beyond vegetables, as people decide that fruit have feelings too.

The movement will start early next century when botanical research reveals that plants cry when they hear sad music and flowers shriek when they are picked. Within months, a new movement will emerge that considers displaying a vase of cut chrysanthemums to be as insensitive as moose antlers over the fireplace.

The new purists will demand that people eat only rotten vegetables. Within years a vegetable liberation front (VLF) will form and condemn the harvest as an annual massacre, as savage as the buffalo hunt.

An aging Brigitte Bardot's followers will throw themselves in the path of lawn mowers to save ragweed, purple loosestrife and stinging nettles. There will be underground books, starting with *The Complete Inorganic Gardener: How to Raise Stones in Your Backyard*. It will be followed by a re-issue of *The Whole Earth Cookbook*, with recipes using only dirt, and then *The Joy of Cooking Mud*.

Within decades, there will be a new crop of fast-food chain restaurants, where they serve loamfries instead of homefries, along with the McMud Burger.

By the year 2100, there will be elegant dining room menus, like this one:

ROCK OF AGES
RESTAURANT

TABLE D'HÔTE

Served at your table:
One fresh table grilled to charcoal perfection,
in your choice of melamine, Formica or marble.
For omnivores, also available in tasty oak.
50,000,000 beavers can't be wrong!

•

Recycled Rigatoni

Creamy coaxial cables served al dente in a pentium pesto sauce,
lightly sprinkled with nuts and bolts.
Served with an entree of 8-track tape tostada
or our famous Microchips 'n' Dips.
Waste not want not.

•

Mississippi Mama's Mud Pie

Sediment from the Mississippi Delta baked to a crunch.
Choose from toppings of freshly churned Portland cement,
ferrous fudge or a scoop of Mud à la mode.
Fresh from Mother Earth.

•

100% Fat-Free

Top 20 Headlines of the Millennium

by Charles Gordon

In the next 2000 years, the news media will be forced to adapt to a rapidly changing world and the rapidly changing world will be forced to adapt to the news media. Here are the top 20 headlines you can expect in the next Millennium…

Worldwide manhunt for perpetrator of Millennium Bug hoax

Asia and Europe merge to form new continent

Ken Griffey III signs $12-billion Euro contract

New continent develops parking shortage

Alaska becomes Disney theme park

Man bites dog

Climate change exaggerated, Sahara Lake conference told

Russia to merge with Canada, Disney announces

Year 3000 will actually occur in year 3001: expert

Stock market hits new low
War clouds loom
Stock market hits new high
Phone sex banned
Fax sex looms

President admits marital sex

Outbreak of marital sex looms

Disney bans marital sex in Alaska
Oswald denies shooting Elvis

Unidentified flying objects identified

Image of Monica Lewinsky spotted at Grassy Knoll

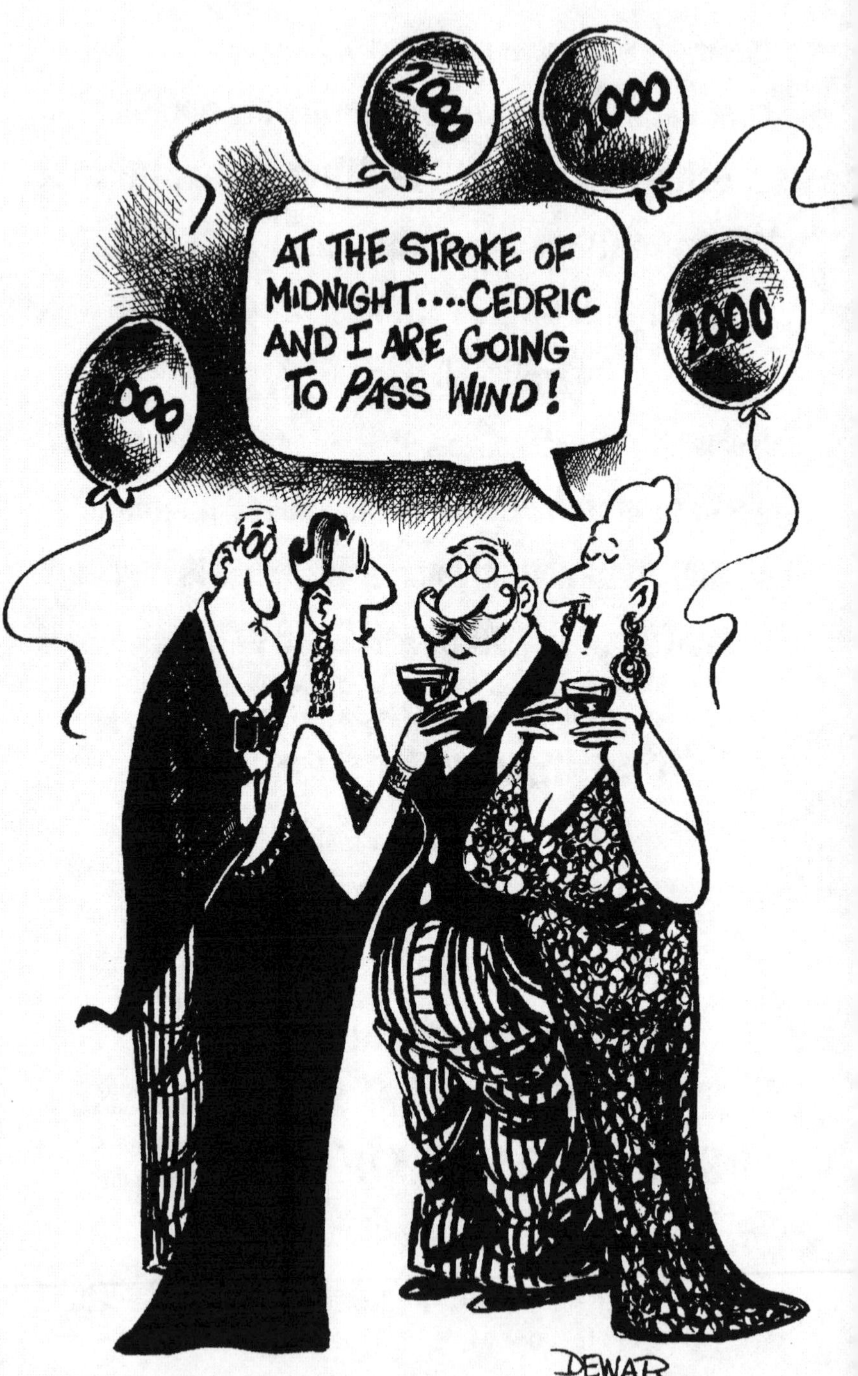
2000
2000
2000
AT THE STROKE OF MIDNIGHT....CEDRIC AND I ARE GOING TO PASS WIND!
DEWAR

Gable

Y2NIGHT!

2

THE BIG MOMENT

No matter what precautions you've taken, it will be hard to hide from the hoopla when the Big Night arrives.
So unless you're spending Dec. 31 in a cave, here is some advice on how to survive the final minutes and have a moment to call your own.

THE MOTHER OF ALL MOMENTS

by Albert Nerenberg

The worst thing about the big moment is the pressure to get it right, even if all you're trying to do is ignore it. This is a moment you don't really want to screw up, because you won't get a second chance for 1000 years.

Here are some perils to avoid to make sure your moment isn't disastrous.

DON'T:

- Yawn during the exact moment
- Die from excitement leading up to the moment
- Have something on your teeth at the exact moment
- Be in the bathroom taking a leak during the moment
- Experience the moment with the wrong person
- Say something stupid right before or during the moment
- Be the only person in the room no one is kissing at the moment
- Be stuck in traffic on your way to a party to celebrate the moment
- Get slobbered on by a drunk you're standing next to at the moment
- Have your watch stop working just before the moment

Whatever you do during the moment, you're likely to suffer Moment Envy: the sense that people elsewhere are having more important moments than you. In the days following the moment, people will do their best to make you believe they had a more momentous moment than you.

Your memory of the moment will be competing with "Fred and I had the most absolutely perfect moment in Bali," or "we had a magical moment at Harry and Thelma's champagne and charade party."

Your only consolation will be that your paltry moment sounds like someone else's paradise – providing you describe it with the right amount of drama. So make the most of your moment, whatever it involves.

Gable

How to
Celebrate the Millennium
if You're a:

MOVIE STAR
- Get your hair done 2000 times
- Have 2000 facelifts
- Give 2000 gowns to charity

ATHLETE
- Sign 2000 baseballs
- Make 2000 changes in your contract
- Store 2000 urine samples in the freezer

CONSERVATIVE
- Fire 2000 employees
- Cut down 2000 trees
- Take a $2000 tax exemption
- Evict 2000 tenants

DICTATOR
- Execute 2000 dissidents
- Burn 2000 books
- Buy 2000 virgins
- Explode 2000 nuclear warheads

MASOCHIST
- Smoke 2000 cigarettes
- Get spanked 2000 times
- Tape all stations on Millennium eve and play them over, and over, and over...

LIBERAL
- Give $2000 to a squeegee kid
- Give the squeegee kid a lecture about 2000 things he should do with his life
- Adopt 2000 third-world children: send each a boxed set of Joan Baez CDs

POLITICIAN
- Kiss 2000 babies
- Break 2000 promises
- Take a $2000 bribe
- Steal 2000 votes

POLICEMAN
- Issue 2000 parking tickets
- Eat 2000 donuts
- Arrest 2000 criminals

LAWYER
- Bill 2000 hours
- Plea bargain 2000 down to 1930

SINNER
- Say 2000 "Hail Marys"

SAINT
- Save 2000 sinners
- Buy 2000 people a coffee

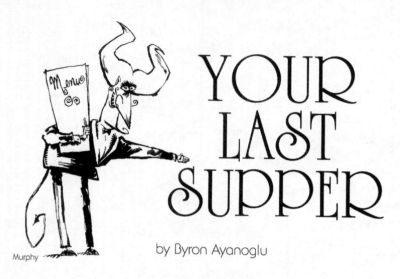

YOUR LAST SUPPER

by Byron Ayanoglu

Murphy

The big night draws near and a nagging question gnaws at your mind. Is the world going to end at midnight, Dec. 31, 1999?

There is no convincing reason to expect a sudden end to the planet, but then again, Jesus treated his Last Supper as just another meal with the Disciples and look what happened to him.

It's important for you to decide one way or the other, because if this really is your last supper, you should plan a meal to end all meals.

You could do something festive, but is that really appropriate? And anyway, why slave over a hot stove during what could be your final few hours on Earth? No, it should be a meal just for yourself. Something simple, but simply divine. Let's say, a sandwich. A sandwich to die for – but which one?

MENU 1: A HEAPING HISTORICAL HERO

Porcupine livers – The most delicious of road kill

Mangosteen fruit – Queen Victoria's favorite

Lark's tongues – Good enough for the Romans, good enough for you

Perigord truffles – The feast of the Bourbon dynasty

Caspian black caviar – The Tsar's last meal

In case there's no time for dessert, add *Belgian chocolates* melted on top. (Who's counting calories at a time like this?)

This will be a disgusting combination, and cause much heartburn, but when your remains are unearthed in another 2000 years, they'll reveal gastronomic trace-evidence of the best edibles of our time.

MENU 2: A BACK-TO-BIBILICAL BAGEL

For something less ambitious, try a modern global version of the "loaves and fishes" meal made famous by the Host of the first Last Supper. Make a smoked salmon sandwich that's traditional, yet international. For instance:

Scottish smoked salmon

Capers from Provence

Vidalia onions from Louisiana

Lemons from the Bahamas

Cream butter from New Delhi

Dill from the summer fields of Suffolk

New York bagel

But maybe this is sounding like too much work again. And who wants to greet the end of the world in a sweat? Simple. Keep it simple.

MENU 3: A FRUGAL FINAL FOCACCIA

Armageddon Lite: No Bourbons, no Bahamas, no butter, no fun.

Plain focaccia

Served with no champagne, just some Evian water. Not much and not chilled. Eat it by yourself in front of the TV. Go to bed early.

If you wake up the next morning and the world is still intact, then have a fabulous New Millennium brunch. And break open the champagne. If you don't wake up because the world has ended, at least you'll have had a good night's sleep.

And you won't have indigestion.

LAST CALL

Here are some cocktails for the daring drinker on the night to end all nights:

- **Mead-Your-Maker:** 2000-year-old home brew, for the hangover of the Millennium.
- **The Cold Warrior:** alternate shots of Jack Daniel's and frozen Stolichnaya, until bombed.
- **The Manhattan Project:** 2 parts uranium mixed rapidly in a particle accelerator. Stir till fission.
- **Huntsville Hemlock:** a lethal injection of Southern Comfort and cyanide.
- **Armageddon-Out-A-Here**: sterno, wood alcohol, shoe polish and vodka. Drink till dead.
- **Y2Kevorkian:** the doctor's favorite cocktail, served up in either a 60-minute or 10-second time-release capsule.
- **Doomsday Die-Just-Stiff:** equal parts Viagra and formaldehyde.
- **Millennium Molotov Cocktail:** prepare as usual. Light. Drink, don't throw.
- **Bloody Caesar:** take one emperor, stab repeatedly, strain and serve.
- **Bloody Mary:** one Scottish queen, one ax, one glass. Execute well.
- **Bloody Glove:** everyone knows how it's made.
- **2000 Sunrise:** both a celebration (the world didn't end at midnight) and a hangover cure. Two shots tequila, a splash of Grenadine, four Tylenol.

MILLENNIUM EVE RESOLUTION
Lose weight by Y3K

ENTERTAINMENT 2NIGHT

by Mike Boone

You've avoided the Millennium Eve party of the nerd next door. It's too dangerous to go out on the streets what with planes falling from the sky. Face it, it's you and the tube.

But what to watch? Here are our pick hits for a Millennial evening, bathed in the white glow of the only friend who's always there.

2	**PET CHANNEL**	**Your Friend the Millipede**
3	**NBC**	**NY2K BLUE:** Sipowicz tries to crack a mass suicide in Times Square
8	**CBS**	**Dr. Quinn, Millennium woman:** Jane treats an epidemic of saddle sores on the frontier of the new century
9	**FOOD CHANNEL**	**Best Recipes of All Time:** including "How to Microwave a Mastodon"
10	**INFOMMERCIAL CHANNEL**	**How to lose 2000 pounds**
13	**ETHNIC TV**	**Serbian Cooking:** Dusan Petrovic, author of *2000 Tasty Things You Can Do with a Croat*
14	**VH1**	**The Eagles' Millennium Reunion**
15	**Very VHI**	**Perry Como Sings 2000 Favorites**
16	**CNN**	**Larry King Live:** Interviews with the top 10 Dead People of all time
18	**FOX**	**The Simpsons Millennium Special:** Sideshow Bob is exposed as the Anti-Krusty
20	**FAMILY CHANNEL**	**A Disney Millennium:** Kasey the K-9
21	**DISCOVERY**	**20,001 Leagues Under The Sea,** followed by **"Climbing K-2 on YK2"**
25	**ESPN**	**Finale of Evil vs. Good:** Ultimate Fighting Tournament: Mike Tyson vs. the Dalai Lama
26	**NICK AT NITE**	**Mary Tyler Moore Millennium Marathon**

27	**OUTDOOR LIFE**	**Armageddon Camping:** "2000 ways to cook a cockroach by candlelight"
29	**BRAVO**	**Mllnm Thtr:** Avant-garde play in which the scrpt hs n vwls
30	**PBS**	**The Crusades:** Debut of 88-hour Ken Burns' series
31	**PLAYBOY**	**Millennium Movies:** I Want to Make Tea with Your Panties, 1984 Hungarian sex farce (sub-titled)
33	**LIFETIME**	**Martha's Millennium:** How 2 K-ter a Y2K Party
35	**CHRISTIAN TV**	**Happy Birthday, Jesus** and other favorite tunes of the Millennium
46	**HISTORY CHANNEL**	**This Hour Has 2000 Years:** A brief history of the last 20 centuries, including the acclaimed: "The Renaissance in Nine Seconds" and an animated version of the "Hundred Years' War"
47	**BBC**	**From England:** That Was The Millennium That Was
48	**WDR**	**From Germany:** That was The Millennium That Wasn't
49	**CRZ CHINA TV**	This Is The Millennium That's Ours
50	**WGAL INDIA TV**	That's What You Think
51	**MOS RUSSIA TV**	From the Mongols to Marx to the Mafia: 1000 years of Misery
53	**SHAW IRAN TV**	Celebrating the Year 1377
54	**FRANCE TV**	1000 Years of Unmitigated Gaul
58	**DESSERT CHANNEL**	1000 Ways to Make a Millefeuille
61	**YTV**	**Are You Afraid of the Millennium?** A panel of teens agrees, "Whatever…Totally"

Not 2night, Dear

Friday night, 11:57

by Richard Martineau

Bado

You refuse to do the same thing as everybody else – go to a mega-party on a tropical island, or rent an igloo in the middle of Iceland. You want to escape the madness, the insanity. So you decide to stay home, with your partner. And here you are, at 11:57 p.m. on Dec. 31, 1999, sitting quietly in the living room, with a glass of champagne in your hand, waiting for the Millennium to end.

> – *So, here we are.*
>
> – *Yeah, it's almost time.*
>
> – *The big moment.*
>
> – *Yeah.*
>
> – *You know, the other day, I was thinking how cool it would be to begin the new Millennium by making love. It'd be like a second birth – the ultimate orgasm, our own personal Big Bang. The big fetus floating in the sky, a Strauss waltz blasted in the living room, my spaceship entering your orbital station... Don't you think?*
>
> – *Euh... yeah, whatever...*
>
> – *What? You prefer watching Dick Clark on TV?*
>
> – *No, no, it's not that...*
>
> – *Then what?*
>
> – *Well... It's that time of the month. Tomorrow or Sunday, it'll be okay.*

– *What, tomorrow or Sunday?! The Millennium ends in three minutes, for God's sake! Tomorrow, it'll all be over; it'll be a day like any other day: Saturday, January the first, The Rose Parade, the kids, your sister and her crazy husband! The magic will be gone; the Millennium will be history!*

– *I can't believe you're making such a fuss about the goddamn moment. You were the one who said it didn't matter. That's why you didn't want to go with Jane and Leo on the big trip.*

– *Well... they were making too much out of it.*

– *Yeah? Well, do you know where Jane and Leo are at this very minute? Not in their apartment, in front of the TV. Not in their condo in South Beach. But in Venice, Italy!*

– *Big deal. Half the human race is in Venice, Italy. I bet there's more space in our living room than in Italy, Germany and France combined. Besides, who wants to begin the 21st century in a dying city? Wagner died in Venice, Marco Polo died in Venice, Thomas Mann wrote* Death in Venice... *Ever read* Death in Denver? *No, never. Want to know why? Because nobody wrote it, that's why, because Denver is all about birth, beginning, discovery, and not death.*

The clock strikes twelve times. You watch each other in silence.

– *So, I guess maybe I can do it. You want to?*

– *No, forget it, I'm not in the mood anymore. Anyway, it's too damn late.*

– *Yeah, I'm not in the mood either.*

You turn on the TV. Dick Clark is crying in the middle of Times Square. Four million people are singing and screaming and hugging each other. A big 2000 flashes on the screen.

– *How old is Dick Clark, anyway?*

– *I don't know and I couldn't care less...*
  Happy 21st, Phillip.

– *Yeah, Susan, Happy 21st.*

A MILLENNIUM TO DIE FOR

by David Sherman

Murphy

Roughly two billion Earthlings have died since Jesus was born. In the next Millennium, another 790 billion people are going to be felled by flesh-eating disease, ax-murderers, Sunday drivers, faulty tires, war, famine, pestilence and jealous lovers.

If you hope to distinguish yourself from this anonymous mass of humanity, you'll have to act fast. Because this is the perfect time to die.

Why not make yourself a celebrity by becoming the very first fatality of the new Millennium? If you can hit the floor as the clock strikes midnight on Dec. 31, 1999 and stay there, you'll make headlines and go down in history.

To beat the crowds, you'll have to design your death carefully. With all the Millennium partying going on, thousands of fools will be biting the biscuit inadvertently around midnight, while lighting Roman candles or careening home drunk.

To make sure you're noticed, you'll have to pass with panache. Here are some suggestions for how to design your own personalized doomsday – thereby achieving a certain immortality.

At least in the record books.

THE LONG GOODBYE

Jumping out of an airplane, minus a parachute, is buying it with bravado. Done right, you'll meet the ground with sufficient impact to meet your maker right at the stroke of Millennium midnight.

Caution: Poor night navigation could cause you to hit water instead of land and spend the New Year unnoticed by anyone but fish. To really make a splash, aim for Times Square during the countdown, though this being New York, there's a chance you'll be ignored.

You will, however, leave a lasting stain.

DYING OF PLEASURE

This is for the serious hedonist who wants to soak up life's pleasures before the final exit. You've still got a few months left till Dec. 31, 1999 – more than enough to kill yourself by liver failure, lung cancer or even cholesterol.

All you need are some credits cards, single malt scotch and Marlboros. Start by maxing out your credit cards on fatty meats and creamy sauces – if your plan goes right, you and your card will have expired by the time the bill collectors arrive.

To make sure, kill the scotch while it kills you. And the Marlboros? Well, have you seen the Marlboro man lately?

If timed properly, just as everyone starts singing the first bars of "Auld Lang Syne," your heirs will be calling the tabloids with the good news.

IT TAKES TWO TO DIE

This is the perfect option for cowards, as well as those who want a sense of tradition in their trek to eternity. For instance: enlist a buddy and plan a midnight duel. Pistols will allow you to be counting paces while the rest of the continent is counting down seconds.

If you can't find a friend to fight, there's always the traditional lion option, in keeping with the holiday's Christian roots. This may involve some pain, but headline-writers are sure to lionize you.

For a more contemporary spin, you can duel with cars, yachts – or even Seadoos, as long as you miss the boat until midnight.

Caution: If you're duelling with cars, remember – the best airbag loses.

DEATHSTYLES OF THE RICH AND FAMOUS

Join the plutocrats at Aspen or St. Moritz for a lovely New Year's suicide on skis. Some hills are lighted, ideal to videotape your final descent for the

New Year's Day news. Performing a 10-point Kennedy/Bono Tree Hug may require serious substance abuse, but that will only put you on an even keel with many other out-of-control revelers.

Caution: Several other jetsetters may unintentionally ski through a tree before the appointed hour, and could take you down with them. So remember to ski safely, if you want to stay alive long enough to die at midnight.

Break a leg.

Legal Advisory: This story is not to be taken seriously. The last thing we want is the first lawsuit of the Millennium.

"...and he was always the life of the party."

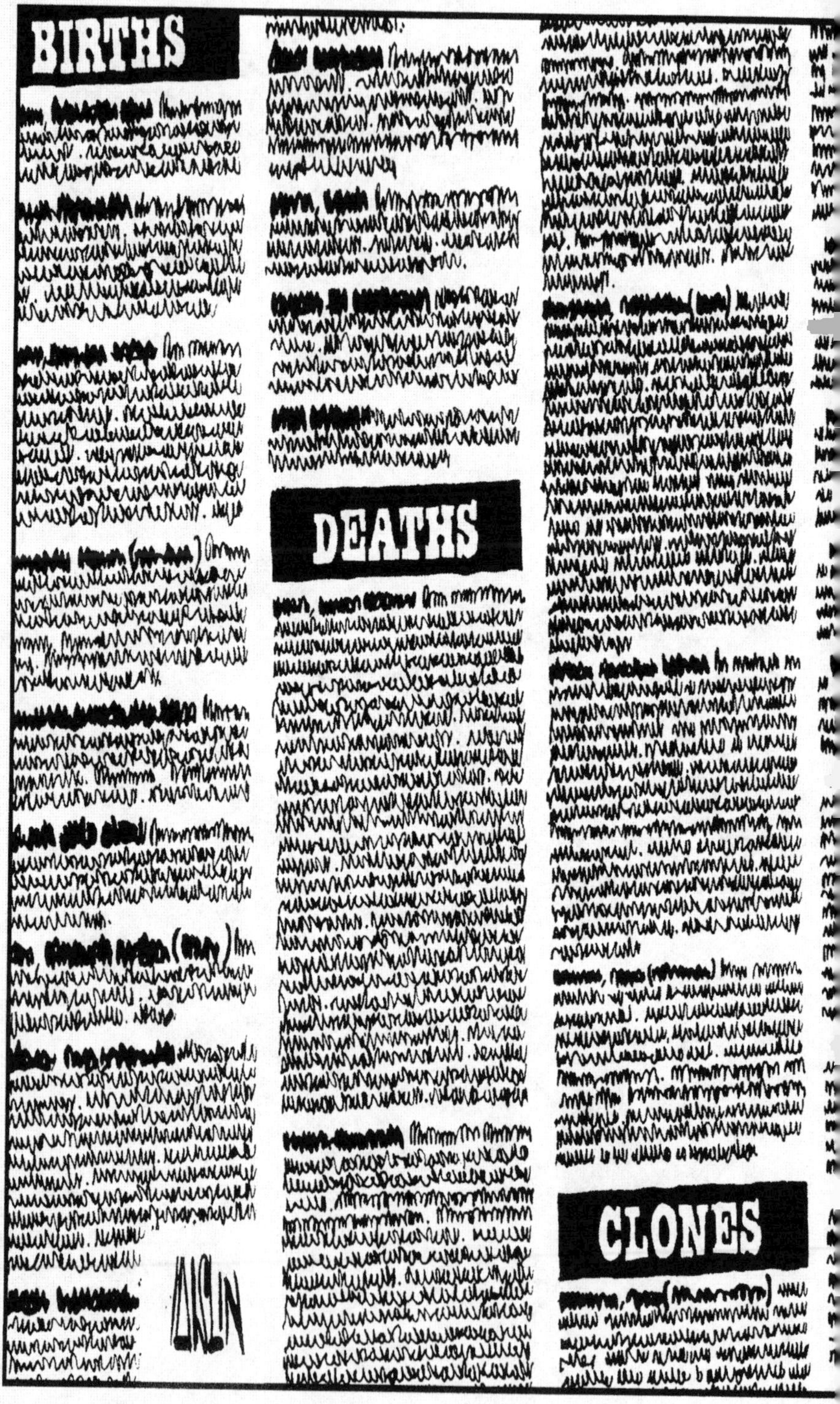
BIRTHS
DEATHS
CLONES

Gable

Y3K

1

Planning your next Millennium

As historians pick over the bones of the last 1000 years, futurologists are already predicting what awaits us in the next 1000 – like nose-ring cell phones.

But what you need is practical information: a comprehensive guide to that challenging destination called the next Millennium, a handy handbook to suit a range of budgets.

What you need is…

Y3K
THE CROWDED PLANET GUIDE TO THE NEXT MILLENNIUM

by André Picard

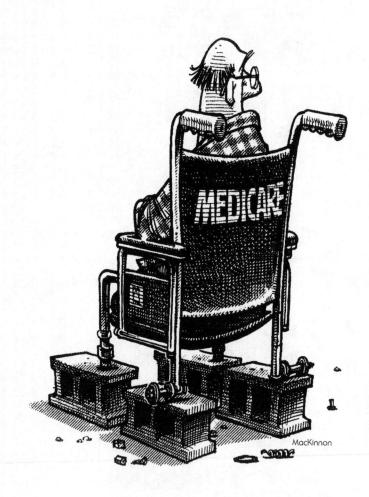

Well, travelers, you've made it. By the time you get to this chapter, the Millennium celebrations may have come and gone without any bugs – and with luck, you're not reading this book by kerosene lantern.

It's time to start looking ahead.

On Jan. 1, 2000, take a minute to throw out your recycling bin full of advertising flyers for Snowblaster 2000 and raise a toast to all those poor souls who spent the previous evening getting seasick on an overpriced cruise.

But take only a minute. The future beckons – and Year 3000 is only 365,249 days away.

With new advances in medicine, you can't be sure you won't be around for trillennial Millennium hype.

Those who have survived Year 2000 festivities know that it's never too early to start trotting out the excuses.

"Dec. 31, 2999? Oh, geez, sorry, I can't make your party. That's the night my wife and I are will be on the third moon of Jupiter for a Rocky Horror Picture Show 1025th anniversary party."

Gable

So, here is a mini-survival guide to the Year 3000. If it whets your appetite, get your order in early for *3000 Reasons to Hate the Trillennium*.

Looking ahead, here's what you need to know about the next 1000 years:

CLIMATE

Hot and bothersome. The enormous quantities of fireworks set off to mark the arrival of Year 2000 have speeded global warming and ensured that, by Year 3000, the hole in the ozone layer will be the size of Pluto. So, stock up on Sunblock 3000 and asbestos bathing suits, just in case there are any lakes left.

FLORA AND FAUNA

If you think this Millennium bug was big, just wait till you see the next one...

Mayes

ECONOMY

In 1000 years there will be only one corporation – Macrosoft.

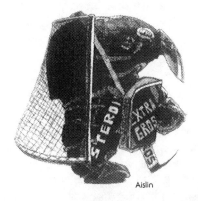

Aislin

SPORTS

The one-minute mile will be mundane, but weightless wrestling will make a comeback.

The first Bulgarian Sumo goaltender will have a 50 shutout season because her pads block the whole net.

DANGERS AND ANNOYANCES

Rapidly receding shorelines and advancing deserts.

ACCOMMODATION

There was a time when the US government was troubled by the fact school kids weren't eating any vegetables. They solved that problem by declaring ketchup a vegetable.

A similar solution is in order for housing. Just think of the sky as your roof, a break in the smog as your window...

Ah, home sweet home.

ENTERTAINMENT

Virtual movies remain big, and hopes are high for a scratch and bleed version of Millennium III: Jesus' Revenge.

MEDICAL

Brace yourself for the drive-in, self-serve hospital. Feeling queasy and stuffed up? Just pull over to your nearest Automatic Doctor Machine (ADM), slip in a credit card, then slip in an arm for blood tests.

The machine will mumble the usual bland re-assurances, then issue a prescription. If more tests are needed, it will provide a little sample bottle to fill up in the comfort of your car.

GIFTS AND SOUVENIRS

The early buzz is that Windows 2098 is a must-have although it's not Y3K-compliant with less than 3 trillion gigabytes. During the coming lull between Millenniums, the prudent shopper can score some "The End is Nigh" beach towels and T-shirts saying "My mother went to Tonga and all I got was this lousy..."

GETTING THERE

There still won't be any personal jet-packs, flying cars or moving sidewalks (except in airports), but the tricycle will break the sound barrier.

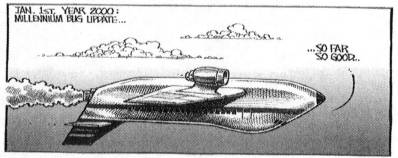

JAN. 1ST. YEAR 2000: MILLENNIUM BUG UPDATE...

...SO FAR SO GOOD..

MacKinnon

FINAL TIP

It's never too early to start thinking about getting copyrights for 3000.

A MILLIPOEM

by Willa Marcus

In a world gone mad for things millennial,
Some prefixes will be scorned as centennial.

"Tri" from triennial, "sesqui"-centennial,
And most of all, humble "bi"-centennial.

Biweekly, biannual, biennial will die,
Like other such bi words, they'll all go bye-bye.

Bye-bye bipartisan, bisexual, bilingual,
Bifocals, bisexual and even the bicycle.

All bypassed. All millified.

The fate of words once common and perennial,
Now swept away in bilious – oops – millious,
Disdain for the unmillennial.

Shudder. And prepare.

For milliathalon, millimonthly, millinocular,
Millichloride, millisexual and millipolar.

Thank goodness, at least some words will remain.
Just as they were, without being renamed.

For example, there's millipede and millinery,
And there's millefeuille, and military,
And then there's the city of Milliwaukee,
And Milly Gosh, there's the Milliky Way.

by Milla Warcus (formerly known as Willa Marcus)

Predictions for the New Millennium

by Dave MacDonald, Marsha Boulton and Gordon Snell

Aislin

- Traffic in the new Millennium will be so bad that researchers will identify a condition called "Driveway Rage."

- Some unscrupulous 7-11 Stores will recycle Twinkies that expired in 1900.

- Thanks to the number of baby boomers passing through menopause, global warming will be far more of a problem than predicted.

- Not far into the next Millennium, people who wear their hats backward will finally turn them forward to face the future.

- For the first time, you will mis-date a check by 100 years.

- The Y2K Bug Law: All financial discrepancies in your account resulting from the change to the Year 2000 will be debited to your account.

- The Y2K Bug Corollary: All financial discrepancies in Bill Gates' account resulting from the change to the Year 2000 will be debited to your account.

- Get ready for the Gravestone bug. There will be a crisis for all of the people who bought order-in-advance gravestones with their birthdate and a death date starting 19–...
Cemeteries are reportedly filled with them, and they all crash at midnight, Dec. 31, 1999.

- It would not be a good thing to put the remote control device for your TV into a Millennium capsule because you would miss out on watching television for the rest of your life.

- If aliens from outer space use their space craft to flatten the grass in some farmer's field and spell out "2000", you will have to ask yourself: "How did they know what year it was?"

- If scientists come up with a cure for muscular dystrophy in the year 2000, there won't be any Jerry Lewis Telethons in the next Millennium.

- If you believe the Doomsday scenarios of many cults, airports will have a lot fewer people pestering you with their literature.

- If the Jehovah's Witnesses are right, the world will end the day your mortgage runs out.

- If the Aztecs are right and time is cyclical, we may have to go through this all over again.

**The Doomsday men gave me a fright
When they said, "On Millennium night
The whole world my friend
Will come to an end."
But how will they know if they're right?**

OH, NO...

by Jack Todd

A new decade is coming and what will it be called?
We had the roaring twenties, the dirty thirties,
the fab fifties, the swinging sixties,
the "me decade" eighties and the nasty nineties.

But what will we call the 00s? Some suggestions:

The Ohs

The Oh-Ohs

The Uh-Ohs

The Big Os

The Double Os

The Oughts

The Noughts

The Ought-Noughts

The Zeros

The Zips

The Goose Eggs

BALLAD OF THE .BUG

(To be whined like a Bob Dylan song)

by Bowser & Blue

Oliphant – Universal Press Syndicate

In nineteen hundred and ninety-one
We were all still cyber-dumb
Unaware of our impending fate
How were we to know back then
That the last decade would end
With the world's worst computer date?

In nineteen hundred and ninety-two,
Bill Gates said: "I know what to do"
Microsoft's the leanest and meanest
And after all, how many shmucks
Can say they made a billion bucks
With a company named after their .penis?

In nineteen hundred and ninety-three
Bill Gates said: "Leave things up to me
Millennium bug talk is absurd
For I can save the human race
By swooping down thru cyber space
I'm your saviour – Super.Nerd."

In nineteen hundred and ninety-four
He claimed we still had six years more
Super.Nerd told us – "Relax!
I am the great computer whiz
I've figured out 2000 is
Just 1994 – plus tax."

In nineteen hundred and ninety-five
.Nerd got stuck in his new hard drive
Millennium fear was quickly mounting
Except in Israel –
Where they said "What the hell!
We're up to Y6K – who's counting?"

In nineteen hundred and ninety-six
We tried to teach old DOS new tricks
.Nerd told us – "Please, have no fear!
Y-2-K will be just fine
If you can think like a K-9
It's 285 dog.years!"

In nineteen hundred and ninety-seven
We all looked back at century eleven
The Dark Ages weren't as dark as we'd heard
Year 1000 didn't break the bank
Their manuscripts did not all go blank
But they had Saint Augustine and we have – .Nerd

"The problem's solved" said Mister Gates
"Here is Windows 98!
The answer's in these bytes and bits
Super.Nerd has finally won
So lemme show you how it's done
I press this button, and – Oh.shit!"

In nineteen hundred and ninety-nine
Super.Nerd searched for a sign
He kneeled in his virtual chapel
And at last, his prayers came true
On the eve of Y2K
Someone bought Bill Gates – an Apple!

Chapleau

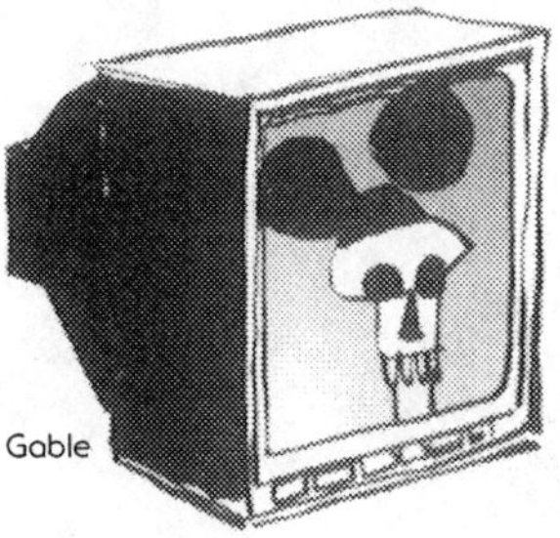

Gable

BOOM...

CHAPTER 0

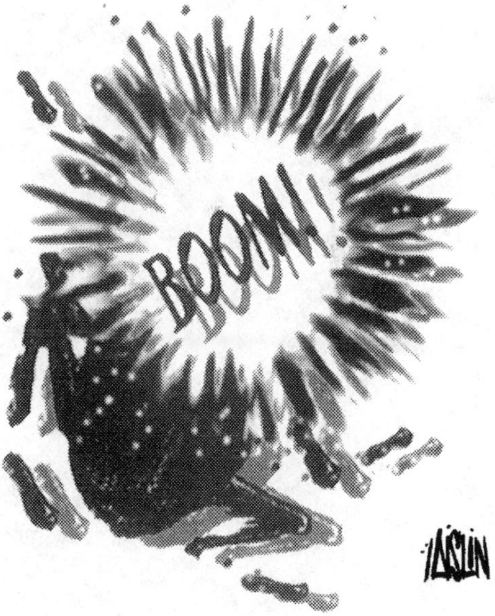
BOOOM!!

If the computer geeks are right,
Times Square at Midnight on December 31, 1999

Josh F